PARENT TRICKS-OF-THE-TRADE

by Kathleen Touw

illustrated by Loel Barr

ACROPOLIS BOOKS LTD.
Washington, D.C. 20009

ACROPOLIS BOOKS LTD.
Colortone Building, 2400 17th St., N.W.
Washington, D.C. 20009

Printed in the United States of America by
COLORTONE PRESS, Creative Graphics Inc.
Washington, D.C. 20009

Library of Congress Cataloging in Publication Data

Touw, Kathleen.
  Parent tricks-of-the-trade.

  Bibliography: p.
  1. Parenting. I. Barr, Loel. II. Title.
HQ755.8.T68   649'.1   81-15021
ISBN 0-87491-086-2   AACR2
ISBN 0-87491-445-0 (pbk.)

PARENT TRICKS-OF-THE-TRADE

"Just the kind of book a busy mother needs. It's succinct, innovative and easy to understand. The drawings will make anybody smile."

—Marguerite Kelly
co-author of *The Mother's Almanac*

Contents

To our children, Steven and Sara; Jessica and Alexander, whose very presence inspired us to find a more efficient way.

To our husbands, Rodger and Bill, whose love, understanding, contributions, and never-ending help with child-care and cooking made this undertaking possible.

A special thank you to:

Our mothers, Mary Jane and Edna for all the ideas they accumulated over the years and passed on to us.

Our children's nursery school teachers, Mary Hagan, Barbara Haney, Marianne Jacobs, Lyn Jensen, Anita Kleinfelter, Monica Myers, Glenda Neal, Sandra Sanchez, and Rhoda Stewert. Their creative ideas made the sections on "Everyday Learning," "Arts, Crafts, and Activities," and "Holiday Crafts" possible.

Deborah Churchman, for the craft recipes from her article, "The Craft of Kids: Glop for All."

Montgomery County librarians, Ann Friedman, Elizabeth Hoke, and Martha Shaw for their help in compiling the bibliography of suggested readings for parents and children.

Martha Shaw, again, for all the time she spent compiling the suggested readings that appear throughout the book.

Michael Messinger for the jacket photo.

Douglas Whatmore, M.D., for the time spent reviewing the "Bumps, Bangs, Moans, and Groans" section.

Donna Datre, Consumer Affairs Manager, Toy Manufacturers of America.

Richard W. Moriarty, M.D., Associate Professor, Pediatrics, University of Pittsburgh, and Director, National Poison Center Network.

James S. Packer, Ph.D., CAE, Executive Director, Association for Childhood Education International.

Jake Einstein, WHFS radio, for permission to reprint recipes from his cookbook, *Homegrown Recipes*, in our "Fun Foods, Naturally" section.

Kathleen Hughes, Marketing Director, Acropolis Books, Ltd., for all her editorial advice, her contributions that added so much to this book, and for her enthusiasm and assistance.

Robert Hickey, Art Department Director, whose proficiency and graphic design skills enhanced this book.

Thanks to all the friends who contributed such good parent tricks-of-the-trade, and an extra special thank you to:

Douglas Whatmore, M.D.

Scott and Berni Bowes
Louise Brown
John and Barbara Carley
Julianne Cline
Dennis and Susan Crawford
Melissa Crisp
Ken and Alice Dalecki
Jan Dollinger
Judy DiVilio
Bob and Naomi Everett
Elizabeth Goodrich
Rita Greco
Jim and Shirley Hammer
Lisa Johnson
John and Kathy Kirk
Arlene Levy

Bill Mattingly
Arlene McGarrity
Michael and Debra Messinger
Reeba Molina
Steve and Stephanie Ney
Susan Peskowitz
Elizabeth Petrovich
John and Kathryn Poletto
Gwen Porcaro
Van and Mary Lee Quinn
Glenda Rhames
Delann Sanchez
Evonne Schnitzer
Tom and Terry Schupbach
Martha Shaw
Ann Sheckells
Gary and Karlan Sick
Katherine Smith
Betsy Spiropoulos
Brook and Sharon Stauffer
Charlotte Sterling
Karl and Dorothy Strittmatter
Sandra Susini
Judy and Pete Taylor
Ruth Touw
Sandy Trupp
Penny Vaden
Doug and Chris Whatmore

A special thanks to our child-testers, too;

Lori and Kimberly Bowes; Lisa, Jennie, Kathy, and Joey Brown; Tod Carley; Emily, Michael, and Leslie Ann Cline; Elizabeth, Ralph, Daniel, Michael, Frank, Jane, and Claire Coscarelli; Casey and Kirsten Crawford; Kevin Crisp; Lizzie, Brennan, Lyndon, and Anne Dalecki; Geoffrey and Bobby DiVilio; David and Jenny Dollinger; Ryan and Brendan Everett; Scott, Christina, and Michael Hammer; Keir Johnson; Rebekah and Erik Kirk; Matthew and Mark McGarrity; Erica and Ari Messinger; Jennifer Molina; Daniel and Benjamin Ney; Benjamin and Joshua Peskowitz; Matthew and Travis Poletto; Stephanie, Anthony, and Alexander Porcaro; Kelley and Kerry Quinn; Monda Rhames; Nelson Sanchez; Karen and Eddie Schupbach; Emily and Andrew Shaw; Kathryn and Reily Sheckells; Gerald, David, and Charles Smith; Erin and Nicholas Spiropoulos; Christian and Hilary Stauffer; Elizabeth and Stephanie Sterling; Mary Kay Strittmatter; Rebecca and John Trupp; Bethany and Kyle Vaden; Jonathan and Katherine Whatmore.

Dear Fellow Parents

During the months we've spent working on *Parent Tricks-of-the-Trade*, we have done a lot of reminiscing about the ways in which we anticipated parenting and the shock of the actual amount of time and work involved in raising children.

Today, the extended family situation has been almost totally replaced by one of shared responsibility by both parents, in which both mother and father take equal responsibility in child-rearing. Even with this cooperation, time becomes a most sought-after treasure; time, not only for ourselves, but with our children; time spent talking, playing, and creating with them.

For more than five years, family and friends shared all the time-saving, money-saving and creative ideas they had accumulated. These hints were all compiled and categorized. They came from both Moms and Dads, new parents and not-so-new ones, families in which both parents worked, and families with full-time mothers or house husbands.

All agreed that it was necessary to find a short-cut to those everyday necessary tasks, especially working parents, whose quality time with their children was extra important to them. Somehow, all contributors had found their own ways to make time for themselves and their families.

The fact that this book exists at all is proof that the time is there, if we can only gain access to it. We did it. Somehow we found the time to write, to rewrite, to collect hints, and to draw. And we produced a book which we hope will enable other frustrated parents to relax a little, and enjoy their children without feeling too rushed. We often worked with babies on our laps and broccoli burning on the stove, but it has all been worth it. In making use of our own advice, and that of families and friends, odious chores became simplified, our anxieties were soothed, and our lives became happier. It's our greatest wish that through reading *Parent Tricks-if-the-Trade,* you too will find that, indeed, life with children can be the pleasure you had anticipated.

The hints in this book are intended to suggest possible solutions only. We cannot guarantee absolute success. Use good judgment when trying them.

For clarification, appropriate age levels, e.g. (3-6 yrs.), have been inserted after certain hints and suggested readings to avoid confusion. Since each child is unique, consider these as general guidelines. (Please note that the abbreviation NB = newborn.)

55 *more* helpful hints on:

While You're Waiting

Make It Easy On Yourself

• Whether or not you plan to have a natural delivery, a childbirth education class will prove to be invaluable when the time comes. It not only helps a new mother to relax and enjoy that important moment, but is also a good place to pick up advice on nursing and care of the newborn.

• Childbirth preparation classes also help new fathers become interested in caring for the baby. A little confidence is *very helpful* when the baby arrives.

• Get a pre-admission form from your hospital. If you fill it out in advance, your hospital arrival will be less hectic.

• Make an appointment to tour your hospital's maternity ward. This will give you an opportunity to see what the ward looks like. Then make a practice run to the hospital. Be sure to time it!

• A relative has offered to come and help out? Wonderful! Convince him or her to come *after* the birth, when you really need extra hands. A guest (and hostess) can get awfully bored waiting for a late delivery.

Perform this exercise as often as possible ↓

• Have your bag packed and ready for your hospital stay. Include the names and phone numbers of friends and relatives who need to be called. Place some change in an envelope in case the new father has to use a pay phone!

• Pack your "goodie bag" for the labor room. Include:

1. Hard candies (Your mouth gets awfully dry.)
2. Lip balm (so do your lips)
3. A stop watch to time the contractions
4. Something for the daddy-to-be to munch on, such as chewing gum or candy
5. A favorite magazine or two for Dad
6. A brush or comb
7. Moist towelettes for freshening up

• Purchase your diapers, formula, and bottles, etc., well in advance so that you do not have to run out for necessities when you should be resting. Give your baby a well-prepared place to come home to.

• Diaper cleaning service should be arranged at this time, too, if you plan to use one.

• A very efficient mother, Terry, suggests you wash and mend outgrown baby clothes friends have given you, long before the due date.

• Before your baby arrives, watch out for sales on baby items. Make a list of things you will need and shop specifically for them. Keep in mind the season and the size your baby will be wearing then. A summer shirt is not a bargain if it fits your little one at Christmas.

• Most mothers-to-be have a difficult time sidling up to the stove during the last month. With some assistance from the father-to-be, cook more food than you need and freeze it. While you are in the hospital your family will eat well; and when you come home you and your husband will have an easier time preparing meals.

• Those old T.V. dinner trays will come in handy to make individual meals with leftovers. Freeze them for quick easy meals for the family. Why not have a supply of T.V. dinners in the freezer instead? Plan menus for the first two weeks at home in advance.

• One of the first things I did before the expected event was to make a list of carry-out restaurants and have their numbers handy. I posted them near the phone.

• Your baby's first weeks are the time to be lazy about dishwashing! Have a supply of paper plates and cups on hand if you don't have a dishwasher.

• Before your due date, hire someone to come in and give your house a "spring cleaning." When you come home from the hospital you'll be able to relax and not worry too much about housework. By the time the dirt has accumulated again, you'll feel ready to tackle it. (Or you'll be hooked on house-cleaners.)

• Do you dread bending your body to scrub that bathtub ring? Use a sponge mop (the kind used to scrub a floor). You'll have no trouble reaching all parts of the tub, and you'll even be able to reach the tile above.

• Use a child's mop to dust in hard-to-reach spots.

• Get yourself ready, not just your house. If you plan to nurse your infant, your breasts should be getting used to the idea before they're called into service. La Leche League can tell you how to toughen your nipples weeks or months ahead of time. For more information on La Leche League, see the section on breastfeeding.

• Have you seen what infant fingers can do to a mass of flowing hair? Now is the time to see what you'd look like with a short, easy-care style.

• Dangle or hoop earrings should be put away. Baby is always reaching and has quite a grip.

• Parents should shop selectively for their pediatrician *before* baby is born.

• Plan to have one of your last "hassle-free" dates. Mom and Dad-to-be should go to one of their favorite spots before baby arrives. Enjoy your night out; don't worry about coming home early for the sitter; sleep in late. Take advantage of this "last chance."

For further advice

Nine Months, by Alice Fleming. (New York: Harper and Row Pubs., Inc., 1972.)

Newborn Beauty: A Complete Beauty, Health and Energy Guide to the Nine Months of Pregnancy and the Nine Months After, by Wende Devlin Gates. (New York: Viking Press, Inc., 1980.)

The Father Book, by Rae Grad, R.N., Ph.D.; Deborah Bash, C.N.M.; Ruth Guyer, Ph.D.; Zoila Acevedo, R.N., Ph.D.; Mary Anne Trause, Ph.D.; Diane Reukauf, M.A.; (Washington: Acropolis Books Ltd., 1981.)

For reference on birth and beyond

The Mother's Almanac, by Marguerite Kelly. (New York: Doubleday & Co., Inc., 1975.)

The Father's Almanac, by S. Adams Sullivan. (New York: Doubleday & Co., Inc., 1980.)

Showers

• Brides-to-be have a bridal registry, so parents-to-be should compile their own baby registry. Let all those friends and relatives know what you need *before* the shower, and you'll save a lot of trips exchanging duplicates.

• At a baby shower, pass around embroidery hoops, cloth diapers, and thread. Have each guest embroider something on the diaper. At the end of the shower, the mother-to-be has a set of diapers that are unique.

• A needle and some colorful thread can also transform baby undershirts.

• If shower guests enjoy needlework, ask each one to bring along a square or two she has embroidered or appliqued, with the initials or name on it. The squares are left with the mother-to-be who can make them into a baby quilt or wall hanging that she will remember long after her baby has grown.

• An "auction" shower can work like this: Each guest brings an article which, though in good condition, she has no more use for. The hostess can play auctioneer and sell the items, with the proceeds going to a savings account for the new baby.

• Purchase thank-you notes and give the guests the envelopes to fill out with their names and addresses. Use these envelopes for a door-prize drawing, then give them to the mom-to-be to use when it's time to mail the thank-yous.

Get the Nursery Ready

• If baby's room will be on the second floor, provide a space on the first floor for napping and changing. Have a bassinet and some diapers, powder, change of clothing, and other necessities downstairs as well as upstairs to save trips up and down the steps.

• A child's shoebag is good for more than just shoes. Usually colorful and cute, they have six or eight pockets which are perfect containers for powder, wipes, lotions, and all those other diaper-changing necessities. Hang the shoe bag next to the changing table, and when your child is older it can serve its original purpose.

Let husband breathe paint fumes.

• Diaper-changing needs can also be within reach when you place a hanging plant basket near the changing table.

• So you wonder where to store those little things—pins, cotton balls, etc.? The sections in an ice cube tray are just the right size.

• Loel suggests hanging a roll of toilet paper on the wall or on the dresser near the changing table. A wipe will always be within easy reach.

• Put a dust ruffle around the bottom of the crib. This will give you extra storage space, and under-the-bed boxes will not be visible.

• A friend suggests lining dresser drawers with giftwrap paper or wallpaper book samples.

• Attach a metal towel rack to the outside of the baby's crib for hanging up blankets when they're not in use. Remove or lower it if your child later decides to use it as a ladder.

• If the mattress is a little small for the crib and it moves from side to side, roll up some bath towels and place them between the mattress and the side of the crib. A gap wider than 2 1/2" is dangerous, as a small infant's head can get caught. This goes for the space between the slats, too, if you're using an older crib.

• Shirley, mother of three, says that anchoring a crib sheet with suspenders will keep it from slipping off.

• She also suggests that those tiny bassinet and cradle sheets can be anchored with the elasticized strap used to hold ironing board covers in place.

• Instead of purchasing crib pads for your child's bed, buy or recycle a full size mattress protector. One can be cut to make two crib pads. After cutting the mattress pad in half, be sure to finish the rough edges.

• Lap pads, made of rubber with a flannel surface, are among those products no new mother should be without. They protect whatever surface you're using for a diaper change, and, when placed under a sleeping baby, save laundering lots of sheets. Great, too, for the laps of well-dressed visitors.

• A piece of foam rubber coverd with oilcloth and placed on top of a dresser makes a good changing table.

• Pillowcases make good sheets for bassinets and cradles as do receiving blankets anchored with suspenders.

• If there is room, put a big comfortable chair in your baby's room. This is a great place for feeding the baby, and later for reading books together. If it rocks, so much the better.

• A very clever Daddy, Bill, put a screen door on his baby's bedroom door in addition to the regular door. This kept pets out, while allowing him to hear and see his child easily.

• Those frequent visits to the bedside of a sleeping child are part of parenthood. To avoid accidentally awakening the baby, install a peephole in the door. You will be able to see if the baby is awake without opening the door.

• A 15-watt bulb in a nursery lamp is bright enough for checking on your child.

• Placemats in animal shapes make inexpensive and cheerful nursery decorations. Tie colorful bibs around the crib. They are fun for a newborn to look at.

• Other popular "eyecatchers" in nurseries are mobiles on the crib and pinwheels in open windows.

• To add sound to the visual, a friend suggests placing a wind chime in the window, too.

• Tie toys together to amuse a small baby. Be sure to use elastic, rather than string, to bind them. Remove these as soon as baby can sit up or reach them.

• Many parents suggest placing a sheet of cork on the wall near the bed. When your newborn becomes fascinated by objects and colors, you can attach different objects and pictures to the board for him to look at. Later, the cork board can be a place to display your toddler's artwork. Watch out for the pins!

• Before purchasing nursery needs consult the *Guide to Buying for Babies* compiled by the editors of *Consumer Reports*. (New York: Warner Books, Inc., 1975.) Or *Good Things for Babies,* by Sandy Jones. (Boston: Houghton Mifflin Co. 1980.)

• For more decorating ideas for children, consult the "Kids' Rooms" section.

95 *more* helpful hints on:

At Home
With Your Newborn

All Day, Everyday
• Those first days home from the hospital are very hectic. Try to take one thing at a time, and get as much sleep as possible.

• The baby's naptime isn't the time for Mom to do the laundry or clean out the refrigerator. Use that time for your own nap—you, too, need rest.

• Betsy, mother of a newborn, avoids naptime interruptions by placing a "Do Not Disturb" sign on her door and taking her phone off the hook.

• Keep a list of things to be done—check them off as soon as they've been completed. (This is also a nice "hint" list for all those helpers who arrive on the scene.) Let them help out while the parents get to know their new arrival.

• If your baby is cranky, take him or her for a ride around the block in the stroller or for a ride in the car. Most parents agree that the motion will lull baby to sleep. Or, just strap your baby into a front-pack carrier next to your warm body and take a walk around the house.

(Keep toes out of mashed potatoes.)

Two methods of dining with a newborn ——→

Napkin

• If it is naptime but your little one is fighting it, sing or hum a lullaby to get baby to relax and fall asleep.

• We've found that baby can also be comforted by: Rhythmic patting, a ticking clock, a recording of your singing, the sound of a heartbeat, the sound of a dishwasher running, or a music box.

• Most childbirth preparation classes suggest placing your baby in the crib, head touching the bumper; he or she will feel more secure and sleep better.

• That handy item, the infant seat, may be of help during those awful hours in the middle of the night when your baby refuses to go back to sleep. I've found that a simple change of sleeping position will do the trick, and I can return to my own cozy pillow.

• Berni, a young mother, suggests putting a dab of your perfume on your baby's crib sheet. He or she will recognize the smell and feel that Mom is nearby.

• An excellent resource for new parents and not-so-new ones is *Baby and Child Care,* by Dr. Benjamin Spock. (New York: Hawthorn Books, 1976.)

The Milk Supply
From the Bottle

• If you don't have room for a lot of bottles in your refrigerator, put the formula into a sterile quart jar. Pour the formula into a sterile bottle before the feeding.

• When you make the formula, prepare a little extra and store it in a sterile container. If you overheat your baby's bottle, cool it off quickly with some of the extra formula in the refrigerator.

• A fast way to heat formula is to make up the bottles with only the concentrate and refrigerate it. When the baby is ready for the bottle, add hot water and shake. This is much easier than reheating the entire bottle of formula.

• A mother in Virginia suggests that instead of purchasing an electric bottle warmer, warm up the bottle in an empty juice or coffee can.

• Whenever you have to be out, carry the measured amount of powdered formula in a container. When it is time to give your baby the bottle, put the formula in the bottle, add water, shake, and the formula is ready and at the right temperature. This is especially handy in the hot summer months when food spoils so quickly.

• Dishwashers can be a timesaver when it comes to sterilizing baby's bottles. According to pediatricians, putting the bottles through a regular dishwasher cycle is a safe method.

• While the bottles are being sterilized, add any other frequently used items to the water such as pacifiers. (Make sure they're things that don't melt.)

• Two very helpful parent suggestions for cleaning bottles are: (1) Use warm water and uncooked rice to scrub out "milk rings." (2) Use baking soda and a bottle brush to remove juice stains.

• Disposable nurser bottles are more expensive but worth the investment since you are assured that the bottles are germ-free.

• Squeeze the bottom of the plastic disposable bottle to remove any air. The air will be released through the nipple and not ingested by your little one.

• To make a hole in the nipple of the bottle, sterilize a needle and place the dull end into a piece of cork. The cork will give you some leverage and save your finger from jabs.

• Crosscut nipples do not clog as quickly as those with holes. You can cross-cut regular nipples with a razor blade. Pinch the nipple, make a cut, then pinch again and make another cut to form an "X".

• If pulp from juices clogs up the nipple of the bottle, put a piece of cheesecloth across the bottle, then screw on the nipple. I've found that this will prevent clogs.

• A "Sit 'n Sip" straw is a very good investment. Your child can drink the bottle without lying down or tipping the bottle.

• An experienced mother, Mary Lee, shares a way to break the bottle habit. She suggests placing a cup of juice on the table next to a bottle of water. See which one your child selects.

• Or, she says, wean your child from the bottle to a cup with a straw. Cut about two or three inches from the straw so that your child won't have to tip the cup to drink. Children love to use a straw, but be prepared for a lot of bubble-blowing, just for fun!

• Put several different colored straws in the cup of milk or juice to add appeal.

• While your child is in the tub, give him or her a training cup filled with a favorite juice. He or she will get practice and if there are any spills, they'll go unnoticed.

• Pacifiers calm colicky babies.

• If your child is really attached to the pacifier, carry a spare around with you in your purse in case one is forgotten or lost.

• Some babies will not accept a pacifier but will suck on the cap and nipple from a bottle. Be sure that you stuff a wad of cotton in the nipple so the baby does not suck air; the cotton must be secure so it can't be removed.

From the Breast
• Cracked nipples are an agony you'll want to avoid. Rubbing them with lanolin or ointments containing vitamins A, D and E helps prevent this, but be sure to wipe the cream off before the baby nurses. Always allow your nipples to dry completely before replacing your nursing pads. Use a hair dryer if you're in a hurry.

• Don't use soap on your breasts when bathing. This dries out the areola and nipple and can contribute to "cracking."

• Try to nurse every two hours. Stimulation increases milk supply.

• Liquids are very important not only when you're trying to build up your milk supply but also during the entire nursing experience. Be sure to drink plenty of fluids.

Brewer's Yeast does great things for your milk supply.

• If your breasts become really full and it's not feeding time, have the baby nurse for a minute or two from each breast. The pressure will be relieved, but the nursing isn't enough to stimulate milk production.

• If you become engorged, some of the pressure can be relieved by placing a cloth-covered heating pad on your breasts. A hot shower is an often-recommended relief, too.

• Most nursing mothers have discovered that certain types of clothing make feeding more private. Wear a T-shirt or sweater rather than a blouse that buttons. You will be less conspicuous. Shawls also provide privacy.

• The right attire is also needed for those nighttime feedings. To avoid struggling to get out the equipment, be sure to have several nightgowns that conveniently open down the center.

• It is recommended that you begin nursing from alternate breasts at each feeding, but who can remember? The standard advice is to keep a safety pin fastened to your bra and to transfer it after each feeding to the opposite breast. In this way, you should know with which breast to begin nursing at the next feeding.

• Before you begin to nurse, use the breathing exercises from your childbirth classes to help you relax. Your milk will let down much faster.

•When your let-down reflex is triggered and it's not mealtime, you can stop the flow by pressing firmly on your breasts with the palm of your hand.

• To ensure that both breasts are emptied at each feeding, nurse five minutes on one side, then switch to the other breast and let the baby nurse as long as he or she wants. At the next feeding begin nursing for only five minutes on the alternate breast.

A relaxing glass of wine or beer will help your milk let down.

• Time to change breasts? Don't pull the breast away. Break the suction first by using your finger to press the breast away from baby's mouth.

• Place the baby on a pillow on your lap while nursing. I've found that this raises the baby just enough to prevent a backache for Mom.

• Before going to bed, a nursing Mom advises getting some magazines out and putting a snack in the refrigerator. When your baby awakens for a night feeding, grab the snack and your baby—the nursing session can be as pleasant for you as it is for your baby.

• No nursing mother will ever forget those early weeks when the baby not only confuses night and day, but wants to eat at least every two hours for an entire *twenty-four* hour period. Rest is very important for you now, so it's time for Dad to get into the act. Prepare a bottle of formula or expressed breast milk in the evening for him to give the baby while you catch up on some sleep.

• If you are going to be away from home for several hours, express your milk and leave it with the babysitter so you won't feel you must rush home for feeding time.

• A working/nursing mother expresses and freezes her breast milk for the times she has to be away.

• A breast-fed baby needs an early acquaintance with a bottle—give him or her one at least twice a week. Acceptance of this form of feeding frees you to go out and makes weaning easier.

• For encouragement, support, and information about breast-feeding, contact La Leche League, a national organization of nursing mothers. Your local chapter can be found in the phone book under La Leche League.

• An excellent book on breastfeeding is *The Womanly Art of Breastfeeding*, published by La Leche League and available through their national office:

> La Leche League
> 9616 Minneapolis Avenue
> Franklin Park, IL 60131

Also

Nursing Your Baby, by Karen Pryor. (New York: Pocket Books, Inc., 1973.)

You Can Breastfeed Your Baby, Even in Special Situations, by Dorothy Brewster. (Emmaus, Pa.: Rodale Press, Inc., 1979.)

Getting the Bubble Up

• These are the successful methods used by parents we know: Before burping, make sure you have a diaper or a flannel lap pad draped over your shoulder. Accidents do happen.

• Seat your child on your lap, tilted forward, chest leaning on one of your hands for support, and pat his or her back.

• Or, reverse this strategy and pat the tummy.

• Hold him or her across one shoulder and pat the lower back.

• Another strategy is to lay the baby on his or her back in your lap, then switch the baby to your shoulder for the burp.

• Vary this by placing the baby across your legs, backside up, and rub his or her back.

Diapering
Cloth Diapers
Reminder: Arrange for diaper service *before* you leave the hospital.

• A friend suggests using diaper liners in your cloth diapers. This not only helps with clean-ups, but also helps to prevent stains.

• Insert the diaper liners as you fold the diapers.

• Flat unfolded diapers are more absorbent than the pre-folded type and are less expensive. If you really want extra absorption and not much bulk, place a pre-folded diaper inside a flat diaper that has been folded in thirds.

• Always double diaper at night. If you have to fuss too much with your baby he or she will be wide awake and ready to play at two in the morning.

• After you wash your diapers, fold the flat diapers into thirds and place the pre-folded diaper inside. This will save time when you need to change your baby's diaper.

• Often a pin will not pierce a cloth diaper. If you run the pin through your hair several times, it will slide right in.

• Brittle plastic pants can be softened by a *brief* tumble in the dryer with a load of towels, or by adding baby oil to the wash to keep them pliable.

• A mug rack on the side of the changing table was an invaluable addition to our nursery. Hang your child's plastic pants here where they are much easier to reach. This is also a good place for wet plastic pants to dry.

Equipment and Techniques
• Keep a large diaper pail in the laundry and a smaller pail in the baby's room. When the smaller pail is full, carry it to the laundry and empty it into the larger pail. You will be able to do diaper laundry less frequently, and will be spared the trouble of carrying a very heavy large pail to the laundry room.

• Place a separate pail next to the toilet for the diapers you rinse in the toilet. No more drippy trails to the baby's room. Or, take the diaper pail lid along to the bathroom, invert it, and catch the drips on the way back to the bedroom.

• Better yet, keep the diaper pail in the bathroom.

• Baking soda or vinegar make excellent deodorizers for your diaper pail and a new toilet brush—for diaper pail only—is just the right size for scrubbing it out.

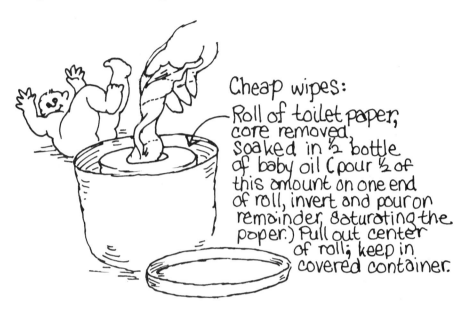

Cheap wipes:
Roll of toilet paper, core removed, soaked in ½ bottle of baby oil (pour ½ of this amount on one end of roll, invert and pour on remainder, saturating the paper.) Pull out center of roll; keep in covered container.

• When your baby is a few months old and becomes more mobile, changing this squirming infant's diaper becomes a wrestling match. To encourage immobility, a parent suggests keeping a basket of stuffed animals near the table for you to grab when baby fidgets.

• If you use cloth diapers, twist the diaper before you lay it flat and pin it. This will provide extra absorbency on top.

• Instead of carrying around a whole box of baby wipes, or purchasing wipes in the convenient but expensive travel pack, take several wipes from your larger box and place them into "zip-lock" bags. They will stay moist and will not take up much space. Some parents prefer to use cotton balls dipped in oil for clean-ups; wet paper towels or washcloths kept in a tightly sealed container are also good.

• An airlines flight bag makes an excellent diaper bag. It is waterproof, there is lots of room inside for everything, and it has a pocket on the outside for additional storage.

• Sometimes it's hard to find small things in a large diaper bag. I keep these small necessities in a make-up bag where they will be easy to locate.

Laundry

• Fill your diaper pail about half-full with water to which you've added Borax, a diaper pre-soak, detergent, or laundry (washing) soda. Rinse B.M.s out in the toilet before soaking them.

• Washing your own diapers isn't a big job, but it requires a lot of button-pushing. First, spin out the pre-soak water. The next cycle should rinse all the residue out, and then you're ready for the actual wash—in hot water. One or two extra rinses ensures total removal of the soap.

• When you wash your child's clothes, wash the diapers first. After the diapers are clean, add the baby's clothing, then wash the clothes and the diapers again. Be sure to add an extra rinse. This will get the diapers really clean.

• Our successful diaper laundry recipe: To remove stains from cloth diapers, mix 1/3 cup dishwashing liquid, 1/3 cup ammonia, and 1/3 cup of water. Put this mixture on the stains and let them dry in the sun. Then wash them with the rest of the diapers. *Don't* use chlorine bleach in addition to the ammonia; poisonous fumes develop when the two are mixed.

• Do not add a fabric softener to your diapers. It decreases their absorbency.

• Adding one cup vinegar to the final rinse will neutralize the ammonia in the baby's urine. It can also take the place of a water softener.

Disposable Diapers

• Buy your disposable diapers by the case or in the large convenience packages. You'll save money and avoid extra trips to the store.

• When your child is tiny and bowel movements are very loose, disposable diapers with gathers around the legs really help prevent leaks. For added protection, or for use with other types of disposable diapers, use plastic pants in addition to the disposable diaper.

• A solution to the problem of a disposable diaper that gaps around the middle is offered by Susan, a friend. She says that she always puts Joshua's diaper on backwards for a snug fit.

• You're sure your baby is ready for a change and rip the adhesive tabs off the diaper only to discover it was a false alarm. A very wise mother says, "Don't discard that diaper—just use masking tape to secure it."

• It's a good idea to carry a roll of tape with you to the pediatrician's office. Again you will not have to discard a clean diaper after the examination—just retape it.

• Recycle those plastice grocery store bags intended for fruits and vegetables. They're perfect for air-tight disposal of paper diapers.

Diaper Rash
• If your child has a bad diaper rash, let him or her soak in a tub of baking soda, wash your child off with an antiseptic soap, dry him or her carefully and apply a lubricating jelly to your child's bottom. Don't apply it too thickly.

• A sunbath not only feels good, it really helps to eliminate a diaper rash. Most pediatricians recommend that you let your little one lie naked on his or her belly in the sunshine, but only for a few minutes. Baby skin is very sensitive. You don't want to trade a diaper rash for sunburn.

• They also recommend that you leave off plastic pants as much as possible.

• Hang diapers on the line in the sunshine to destroy bacteria.

• Since diaper services sterilize diapers, a child's rash is less likely to become aggravated. Consider it.

• It has been determined that most babies who wear disposable diapers seem to have less problem with diaper rash. Try switching to disposables to see if it makes a difference.

• Cranberry juice has a neutralizing effect on urine. My friend, Kathryn, served it often to her diaper-rash prone little one.

79 *more* helpful hints on:

Body Care

Bath Time

The Newborn

• A bath right before bedtime or naptime may help your child to relax enough to fall asleep easily. But watch out—a bath has the opposite effect on some kids.

• A gentle massage with baby oil before the bath has a very pleasant and soothing effect on babies and small children. Go slowly and gently, and you'll enjoy the experience every bit as much as your little one. Before the bath is also a good time to do simple exercises with an infant.

• Why do we, as new parents, think a baby needs a daily bath? What does he or she do to get dirty? Actually baby's natural body oils lubricate the skin. Occasionally, instead of a bath, put a rubber sheet on the changing table or in the crib and give your child a sponge bath, without soap.

• A kitchen sink is the perfect size for a small baby's bath. A towel in the bottom of the sink will keep baby from slipping. Caution: Be sure the spigot isn't hot to the touch before baby begins the bath.

• It's easier to wash a wobbly little one when both hands are free. A friend suggests placing the baby in a plastic reclining infant seat inside the sink or tub. Don't forget to remove the foam pad and put a towel underneath to prevent slipping. Foam rubber in the bottom of a baby tub also prevents slipping.

• Better yet, when bathing a new baby, wear thin cotton gloves. They help you keep a grip on your slippery little one and save the need of a washcloth.

• I've found that the bathtub is the best place to give your child vitamins. This keeps dribbles and stains off clothing.

Keeping Safe and Happy
• There comes a time when a child is too large for his little plastic tub and too small for the big bathtub. A mother of a young child found that an oval plastic laundry basket placed in the large tub can help ease the transition. Your baby will feel more secure because he or she has something to hold on to. (18 mo.-2 yrs.)

• If your bathroom has a shower stall, another mother's solution for the hesitant bather is to use a plastic inflatable pool there. It will fit easily into the stall and your child will feel privileged to have his or her own mini-bathtub. (9 mo.-3 yrs.)

• Bubble baths are fun, but can leave a child's skin itchy and dry. When this happens, I always add some skin moisturizer or baby oil to the bath water. (Baby oil in the bath water can leave a slimy film. Remove this film easily with a dishwashing detergent which contains a grease remover). (NB-10 yrs.)

• For after-bath efficiency, have a sleeper, undershirt, and a diaper on the changing table so everything will be on hand when you come back to the bedroom to dress your just-washed baby. (NB-3 yrs.)

Getting Clean and Having Fun

• Try to have all your equipment assembled before you begin bathtime maneuvers. It's a good idea to fill a basket with shampoo, lotion, powder, etc., and hang it next to the spot where you bathe your child. (NB-10 yrs.)

Join your baby in the tub for the happiest bath you've ever had.

• Mom or Dad don't need to get a bath when bathing their child. Wear a plastic apron for protection against the "storm" your child enjoys making. (9 mo-5 yrs.)

• Nylon net is the best known substance for scrubbing of very dirty knees and elbows.

• If soap slips out of your child's hand, sew soap scraps or even a bar of soap inside a washcloth. He or she will not have any problems managing it. (3-10 yrs.)

• It's much more fun to have one's bath given by a puppet-friend. Make one out of two washcloths, with three of the sides sewn together. Let the puppet scrub your child, then give your child the puppet and have him or her wash/play for the rest of the bath. (3-6 yrs.)

• Give your child a variety of toys in the bath; water play is delightful. (9 mo-7 yrs.)

• Bathtub toys are wonderful enticements for getting your

children into the tub. too. We always keep our children's toys hanging in a mesh tote in the tub—close-by for use, and easy to dry in their own airy sack when the fun's done.

• Channel wall-painting tendencies by letting him or her decorate the tub area; give your child a plastic container filled with shaving cream and a large paint brush to use to paint the tub and tile. (2-7 yrs.)

• Purchase soap crayons for your child to play with when he or she is in the bathtub. These are a favorite with a lot of toddlers we know, and what's nice is the artwork is easily removed. (18 mo.-6 yrs.)

• An empty squeeze bottle filled with water makes a good bath toy. It's also fun in the outdoor wading pool. (2-6 yrs.)

• Other inexpensive household items that my children enjoy in the tub are: paper cups, funnels, strainers, and sponges. (2-6 yrs.)

• Save soap scraps, melt them, and pour them onto a cookie sheet. When it has hardened somewhat, cut out shapes with a cookie cutter to add some fun to bathtime. An older child can have fun cutting out the shapes. (2-10 yrs.)

• Does your child want to stay in the tub until he or she looks like a raisin? Set a timer, and when it goes off, all play is over. For some reason, it's less painful to obey a timer than a parent. (2-7 yrs.)

• Another encouragement to getting out of the tub is a game of beauty shop. Dry your child off and go to your beauty shop to style his or her hair. (2-7 yrs.)

• With an older child, the problem isn't getting the child out of the tub, but getting him or her in. Why not skip the bath once in a while and wash up in the sink. You'll soon find that you'll be back to the original problem, only now it will be extra long showers and baths, not toys, that keep your child in the bathroom for hours. (7-10 yrs.)

• One mother of boys suggested this approach: She drew pictures of clean people next to unkempt ones. The clean people had smiles and sun rays over their heads. The dirty ones didn't. Her boys enjoyed the pictures and emulated the clean ones. (6-10 yrs.)

Shampoos and Haircuts
• Cold shampoo is a shock to a child in a warm tub. So, we decided to let the plastic bottle float in the bath water. By shampoo time it was just the right temperature. (NB-4 yrs.)

• The baby lotion can float along in the water with the shampoo. It too will be just the right temperature for the after-bath rub. (NB-4 yrs.)

• Have you ever thought of applying shampoo with a sponge? The soap won't run into his or her eyes. (NB-7 yrs.)

• John, a father who frequently is in charge of bath- and shampoo-time suggests that if your child complains about soap in his or her eyes every time you shampoo, buy a diving mask. Your child can keep his or her eyes open and the soap won't get in. For the less adventurous, cover the eyes with a washcloth. (18 mo.-7 yrs.)

• No baby shampoo and your child just poured half the sand-box over his or her head! Use baby soap. It won't burn the eyes either.

• Use a child's watering can to rinse shampooed hair. (NB-7 yrs.)

• Keep children singing while you wash their hair. They'll be too busy to cry and it will make the process seem fun. (4-6 yrs.)

• A plastic reclining infant seat can help a child who is uncomfortable or unable to tilt his or her head back for a shampoo. It will be very easy to rinse your child's head since he or she can't slip over backwards. (NB-1 yr.)

• A rubber hose attached to your bathtub spigot is good for rinsing hair, too. It's also fun to soap up the whole kid and squirt him or her clean with the hose.

• Try having your child lie on his or her back in the tub (in shallow water), hair flowing out around the head. Shampoo floats away. (2-10 yrs.)

• Introduce the older child to the shower. He or she will happily let the spray rinse the shampoo away. (3-10 yrs.)

• When girls begin washing their own hair (and eventually they wash it too much, instead of too little); to check for cleaniness of scalp without offending, play "hairdresser" with them. While you are arranging their hair in some elaborate style, quietly check to see if the hair is clean. (8-10 yrs.)

• In the chilly winter months, I always use my dryer to blow dry my children's hair.

• Hairspray on your brush or comb will eliminate that annoy-ing static electricity.

• My grandfather became the official "barber" for my four brothers. To keep those active boys in one place when they were young, he made them sit in a high chair for their haircuts. They were trapped, and his job was much easier. (9 mo.-3 yrs.)

• Better yet, Arlene, a friend, suggests that you undress your child and do your cutting in the bathtub. Place nylon net over the drain, rinse off all the itchy hair, and you're finished. (18 mo.-10 yrs.)

• To keep hair from getting in your child's eyes when it's being trimmed, let him or her wear a mask. Seated before a mirror, your child will be so interested in how he or she looks, that squirming and complaining will be forgotten. (18 mo.-5 yrs.)

• After a haircut or trim, remove small hair clippings from clothing and neck with your vacuum cleaner attachment.

• Before that big first visit to the barber, turn on Daddy's electric razor and let your son feel the vibration on his neck.

• An often-forgotten resource is the neighborhood barber—for your daughter. If you want a simple cut, you'll save a lot of money.

Nails
• If fingernails and toenails are cut after a bath, they are softer and your job is easier.

• The hospital nursery staff suggests cutting babies' nails while they're asleep. Make sure you have adequate lighting for this procedure! Babies' nails are tiny.

• I've found that a fingernail clipper does a better job than a pair of scissors.

• Cut your toddler's nails while he or she is diverted by a favorite T.V. program. Your child will ignore your ministrations.

• Your older child will like doing his or her own nails. Help with the cutting, then let your child experiment using the nail file or emery board. You may even want to lend some of your clear nail polish. (This is also a good incentive to discourage nail biting.) (5-10 yrs.)

Keeping Teeth Healthy
• Once a baby's teeth come in, the plaque should be kept off. Lay his or her head in your lap, and wipe the teeth and gums with a washcloth. An alternative method is to use your finger, coated lightly with baking soda.

• If you must send your child to bed with a bottle, fill it with water. Any other substance will encourage tooth decay.

• A child should never be given tetracycline, an antibiotic which will permanently stain teeth. Teeth may also be stained in utero if a pregnant mother is given this drug.

• Our dentist suggests placing your child's head in your lap for a more thorough brushing and flossing, since it allows a full view of the mouth.

• Purchase "Floss Fingers." They help support and keep dental floss taut, and make maneuvering a lot easier.

• Most dentists recommend that if you're going to give any high-sugar content food, give it all at once instead of throughout the day. One giant dose followed by brushing isn't as damaging as a continuous dosage.

• Get your child used to the toothbrush early. Give him or her the brush with a little toothpaste on it to get your child used to the taste and to the feel.

• An excellent solution to help your child understand how to brush teeth, is offered by Delann, a friend: She suggests giving your child an explanation, then letting him or her brush your teeth for you. Your child will be able to see into your mouth and will learn how to maneuver the brush.

• An independent child will no doubt insist upon brushing alone. If you doubt your child's ability to do a thorough job, don't argue, compromise. Tell your child to brush your teeth while you brush his or hers. Your child will go along with this and you will be sure that the teeth are clean.

• Or why not let your new brusher do his or her own teeth with the stipulation that you get to check the work. Check with the toothbrush as you say "Oh, here is a spot that you missed," and brush the teeth in those places your child tends to forget.

• Games can solve a lot of problems. Give your child toothbrushes in different colors. Play a guessing game. Try to guess which color toothbrush your child will use for this brushing session. Your independent little one will be sure to select the color you did not choose, but he or she will get started brushing.

• To make sure your child's teeth get more than a cursory swipe, set a timer. Insist that he or she brush until the timer rings. For more fun, put on a favorite record (not a long one, please) and brush to music. No stopping until the record does. You might try using a music box for a change.

• Another child-appealing toothbrushing incentive is to suggest that your child brush his or her teeth in the morning and after lunch, but that it is Mommy or Daddy's turn to help brush at night. Your child gets two turns, but you only get one—the most important one though.

• Some children who won't brush enjoy rinsing out. Somehow, forbidden spitting has a lot of appeal. This isn't as good as brushing, but it's better than doing nothing at all.

• **When all ploys fail to inspire the reluctant brusher, serve nature's toothbrush—foods such as apples, carrots, or celery.**

A Visit to the Dentist

• A dentist's chair can be a little frightening—even to some adults we know! Give your child a pleasant introduction, and both of you will be spared future agonies. Play dentist with your child. Put him or her in a chair with a bib on. Show your child how to rinse out. Tell him or her how the chair moves up and down. Then switch roles. You be the patient this time.

• Take your child along with you when you have your checkup. Your toddler will get to know all the equipment the dentist uses. Seeing the parent have a pleasant time will relieve some of the anxieties about the future visits.

• If your child has been properly introduced to dental procedure at an early age, and proper hygiene is followed, visits to the dentist when he or she is older should be no problem.

Read along with your child

My Friend the Dentist, by Jane Werner Watson, Robert E. Switzer, M.D., Jay Cotter Hirschberg, M.D. (Golden Press, N.Y.: Western Publishing Co., Inc., Racine Wis., 1972.) (3-6 yrs.)

My Dentist, by Harlow Rockwell. (New York: Morrow, William & Co., Inc., 1975.) (3-6 yrs.)

Toilet Training

• Spring and summer are the best seasons for toilet training. With less clothing to remove and the great outdoors to absorb mistakes, your job will be easier.

• With new training pants or pretty panties for a girl, your child will try harder not to soil them. But please, don't scold when accidents do happen.

• A popular potty training trick of many parents is to run water slowly in the sink to make an effective association of sound.

• Don't spend all day in the bathroom. Put your child on the potty periodically, especially a few minutes after eating.

• Try to make mental notes about when your child has a bowel movement. Many parents are amazed by how regular their children are once they decide to keep a record.

• You've figured it out. Your trainee urinates every two hours. Set the alarm for two hours after your latest accident; when it rings, off to the potty.

• Check to see if your child's use of the bathroom coincides with your schedule. When you need to urinate, place your child on the potty to see if he or she will go.

• An often recommended method to help your child make it through the night without an accident is to take him or her to the bathroom before *you* go to bed. (This is one time that it's acceptable to awaken a sleeping child.)

A mother of a cured bedwetter says: "If your child frequently wets the bed, place a rubber sheet and a clean sheet under the regular sheet and waterproof pad. When the inevitable happens, just remove the wet sheet and pad—the bed is already made!" (Could this be the layered look in bedding?)

For additional reading on body care

My Body, How It Works, by Jane Werner Watson, Robert E. Switzer, M.D., Jay Cotter Hirschberg, M.D. (Golden Press, New York,: Western Publishing Co., Inc., Racine Wis., 1972.) (3-6 yrs.)

59 *more* helpful hints on:

Clothing

Infants

• Select colors like white, yellow, or green if you're shopping ahead for clothing. These colors are suitable for boys or girls.

• Infants grow so rapidly that it would be wise to buy a few things and wash more often.

• Pretty as all those "hand wash only" outfits look at your baby shower, they just won't get worn much. You won't be sorry if you exchange them for sleepers and stretch suits. A very frank neighbor specifically requests no fussy clothing when anyone asks about gifts.

• Undershirts with snaps are more practical for a newborn who doesn't like things that pull over the head.

• Cotton clothing will shrink, so buy one size larger to allow for this. Most undershirts and kimonos are made of cotton.

• Booties and socks with elasticized ankles will stay on better than those with ties.

• Pants with snaps at the crotch will make diaper changing easier.

• It's difficult to buy baby clothing in just the right size—sizes vary and your baby may not be a 12-month size when he or she is a year old. Trace around an item of clothing that fits well, and take this with you on shopping trips. You won't have to drag baby along and he or she will be saved dressing and undressing to see if an outfit fits.

Shoes and Socks

• To cover up scuffed shoes, rub a raw potato over the scuff. Then, apply polish. The polish will adhere and cover the scuffed place.

• White shoes are a standard choice, but they require frequent polishing. A baby's shoes don't have to be white. Colored shoes stay clean-looking longer, and may come with a scuff toe in red, brown, or blue.

• Polish patent leather shoes with vaseline or baby oil and rub off any excess. Not only will they shine brightly, but they won't crack.

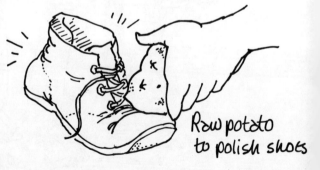

Raw potato to polish shoes

• Whenever my child takes a shortcut across a muddy yard, I use an old toothbrush to get all the dried mess that hardens in the space where the shoe meets the sole.

• Leather shoes won't be damaged if you use nylon net to scrape off dry mud.

• To make white shoes shiny, mix one part white shoe polish to two parts floor wax. Apply to clean shoes; buff when dry.

• It's difficult to keep white shoe polish off the edges of the soles when you apply it. If you paint the edges with clear nail polish, the shoe polish won't adhere.

• Having trouble putting on your child's high-top shoes? Here are ways parents suggest to get him or her to uncurl those toes so the shoe will slide on easily: Tap on the bottom of the shoe; or move the shoe from side to side; or tickle your child behind the knee.

• For some added assistance with shoes, I've always placed my child in a high chair.

• Two excellent tips from our local nursery school are: (1) Tie nylon stockings or plastic bags over your child's shoes, and boots will slip right on. (2) To keep your child's shoestrings from coming untied: double knot or dampen shoelaces before tying.

• To teach your child to tie shoes, let him or her practice with the shoe off, or give your child your shoe to use. Its long laces are easier to manage.

• A friend has found that another easy way to learn is to use two laces of different colors. Show him or her how to make each one into a loop, form an x, then slip one color under the other and pull.

• A child can learn to use a shoe horn. Shoes will wear better longer, and go on easier, too.

• Attach a strip of colored tape to the back of your child's boots so that he or she will be able to identify them easily in the pile of boots at school.

• The most practical tennis shoes have a rubber strip over the toes which prevents your child from ripping the canvas and starting a hole in the toe of the shoe.

• Use dry nylon net to brush-up and clean-up dirty tennis shoes.

• It's hard for a child to put socks on right side up. A very clever Mom suggests rolling each sock down all the way to the heel, so your child can see clearly where the heel is. Then the sock can be pulled on and the top unrolled.

• Tube socks were one of my better discoveries. There is no heel so there is no upside down.

• As soon as you purchase new socks, write the size on the bottom with an indelible marker. The original printing quickly washes away, leaving you baffled when it's time to buy new ones.

• Which socks belong to which kid? This is a laundry problem with a simple solution: Sew a knot in each child's socks with a different colored thread.

P.J.'s
• Buy pajamas with elastic at the ankle for your child. You can also buy a larger size because the elastic in the leg will hold them up. Your child won't trip on extra long legs and you'll get two season's use out of them. (You can also put elastic into too-long p.j.'s yourself).

• Iron-on patches on the feet of your child's pajamas will keep them from wearing out and will help prevent slips.

• Buy p.j.'s that have two rows of snaps. Use the upper row of snaps the first year, the bottom row the second.

• To keep two-piece pajamas from getting separated in the bureau drawer, I always attach the top to the bottom with only one of the snaps.

• Use a coin to pry apart stuck snaps.

• Full-length nightgowns can be dangerous for little girls who climb stairs to their bedrooms. Shorten them to mid-calf length, or buy them a size smaller.

Selection for Independence

• So, your children want to dress themselves? Here are some helpful suggestions from you to them:

Pants go on easier if you're sitting instead of standing.

Sit on the floor to put on your socks.

While you're still on the floor, put on your right shoe first. How do you know? Mommy put a piece of tape inside the right heel.

Put your shirt or blouse flat on a chair or bed, front-side down (or tag on top) before you slide into it.

Pull your head through the neckhole first, then slip your arms in, one at a time. (Reverse this procedure for removal)

To put on a jacket, coat, or open-front top, place it on the floor, front up, with the collar closest to your feet. Bend over, and flip it over your head.

Start buttoning your shirt from bottom to top. You'll make fewer mistakes.

• You can help encourage the independence your child is showing by purchasing clothing that your children can put on themselves. For example, select tops, coats, and jackets with a zipper instead of with buttons or snaps. (3-10 yrs.)

• Pants or skirts with an elastic waist are a good choice. Your child will not outgrow clothing as quickly and will be more independent when dressing or using the bathroom; there's no problem unzipping or snapping. (3-5 yrs.)

• If your child insists on pants with a zipper, buy them, but find some with an elasticized back. Even if he cannot work the zipper, he will be able to slide them off and on easily without unzipping. (3-5 yrs.)

• In addition to dressing without your help, a child also gains feelings of independence and self-worth by shopping for his or her own clothing. Your child's judgment is not likely to be influenced by practicality. Make an initial selection of several items yourself, then let him or her choose from among these. (3-10 yrs.)

• Avoid a bad outfit selection at home by hanging all the clothing up in outfits. When he or she makes a choice, the combination will have your approval and you won't have any reason to criticize. (3-10 yrs.)

• If most of your clothing is kept in drawers rather than on hangers, put plain tops and figured pants in one drawer, plain bottoms and striped and plaid clothing in another. Then your child can make his or her own acceptable selection. (3-10 yrs.)

For additional reading for your child, see
How Do I Put It On? by Shiegeo Watanabe. (Cleveland: Collins, 1979.) (2-5 yrs.)

Care and Repair

• To bring up the nap on velvet clothing, put it into the dryer with a damp cloth for a few minutes and then hang to dry.

• Iron baby's tiny clothes with a traveling iron. It makes the job easier.

• For professional-looking repairs on delicates like little girls' frilly dresses, use iron-on interfacing. It's light-weight and practically invisible.

• My Mom, mother of eight, suggests that as soon as you purchase a pair of jeans for your child, put iron-on patches inside the knees *before* your child wears a hole through them.

• She also recommends a quick way to remove fuzz or lint from clothing: Wrap a piece of masking or cellophane tape around your fingers, sticky side up, and brush over the linty area.

• Turn corduroy inside out before you wash it and it will keep fresh-looking longer. Pressing should also be done from the wrong side so the nap won't be crushed.

Beads (strings won't get lost in hood.)

• Tiny baby socks have a way of disappearing in the wash, only to reappear later in someone's sleeve or in the dark recesses of the dryer. Before washing, I place them in a nylon mesh garment bag—the kind used to wash delicates. The socks will stay together and I don't waste time searching.

• When you must patch a hole in your child's clothing, cut the patch in the shape of an animal before you sew or iron it on.

• Many parents we know buy their daughters' overalls, jeans, and t-shirts in the boys' department. Boys' clothing is better made, sturdier, and will wear better.

• Don't move the buttons on coveralls that are too long. Instead, put new buttons on where they are needed. When your child grows, the original buttons will be ready to use.

• Keep coverall straps in place by crossing the straps in the back and machine stitching a triangle on the spot where they cross.

• Sew buttons on with fishing line. It's stronger than thread so buttons are more resistant to little fingers that are just learning.

• Underclothing seams sometimes scratch and irritate. Have your child wear them inside out. No one will ever know and your child will be more comfortable.

Recycle
• When your child outgrows clothing, pack it away by size and season. When you have a second child or just want to pass the clothing

along to a friend, you will save yourself a lot of time searching through boxes for the right size.

• The wonderful warmth of down jackets doesn't come cheaply. To get your money's worth, buy the coat larger so your child will be able to wear it for two years. It can do duty as a vest if you cut the sleeves off the third year.

• Since children outgrow clothing before it's worn out, clothing in excellent condition can be found at good prices at consignment shops, thrift stores, or yard sales. When frequenting such sales, buy only quality clothing with brand names you know, and check carefully for missing buttons and holes. Also remember to carry along a tape measure and note card with your child's measurements.

• An alternative to yard sales is bartering with friends. Have everyone meet in one location and trade toys, clothing, furniture, and other useful items.

• Our neighborhood has a clothing swap co-operative. Each person in the co-op sews an X inside the items she wishes to contribute; a different color thread is used for each co-op member. She can then begin to trade outgrown clothing for something in her child's size, assured that the color coding will bring her own things back eventually. If she doesn't need the returned clothing for a younger child, she can contribute this article again and select something new for her children from the pool.

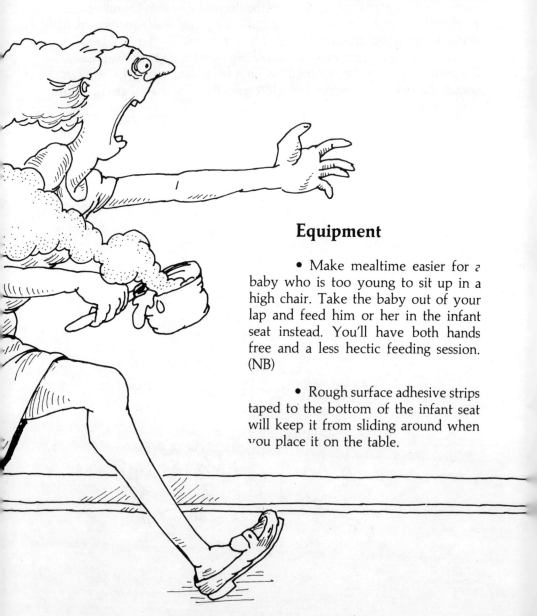

34 *more* helpful hints on:

Mealtime

Equipment

• Make mealtime easier for a baby who is too young to sit up in a high chair. Take the baby out of your lap and feed him or her in the infant seat instead. You'll have both hands free and a less hectic feeding session. (NB)

• Rough surface adhesive strips taped to the bottom of the infant seat will keep it from sliding around when you place it on the table.

• When baby graduates to the high chair, put a rubber mat or foam pad on the seat so he or she won't slide down.

• Instead of tying my daughter's bib at the nape of her neck, I tie it to the side to keep her hair from getting tangled in with the knot. In fact, I've made a simple bib pattern of my own that fastens on the side with snaps.

• Some bib advice: Plastic bibs are much better than cloth ones. They wipe clean, dry quickly, and there's no laundry involved. Plastic bibs with a molded cuff are even better. They wipe off easily and the cuff catches the spills. Disposable foam bibs are great for traveling or eating out.

• A "Sewing Clothing for Children" class offers this idea for homemade bibs: Cut a hole in the center of a hand towel big enough for baby's head and neck to slip through. Decorate with embroidery thread or with sew-on appliques. Or cut a bib shape from a piece of flannel-backed oilcloth and use it for a wipe-clean bib. Use yarn for ties.

• No warming dish? Set aside the pan of water that's just been used to heat baby's bottle. Place the opened jar of baby food inside. While baby drinks the bottle, the slowly cooling water lets the food come to a comfortable temperature. When the bottle is done, the food is ready. (If your prepare your own baby food, put the food in a clean jar or in a training cup without a lid and place inside of the pan.)

First Foods
• It's difficult to feed a fussy child. Distract him or her with a favorite book, preferably one that can be wiped clean, while you spoon in the food.

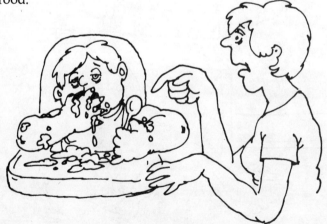

• Don't be discouraged if your child refuses cereal the first time. The feel of a spoon takes getting used to. Give the spoon to him or her while you scoop up the cereal with a zwieback "spoon." The cereal eaten from the familiar teething biscuit is more readily accepted.

• Wooden tongue depressors make good scoops too.

• Instead of giving your child graham crackers or teething biscuits, try puffed rice crackers which contain no preservatives and are low in calories.

• Swallowing is sometimes a problem with a little one just learning. A friend, Naomi, suggests hanging a familiar object such as a toy bird from the ceiling. When her son, Brendan, had trouble swallowing, she had him "look up at the bird." He stretched his neck and the food went down easily.

• Never feed the baby directly from the baby food jar; saliva from the baby's mouth will enter the jar and cause bacteria to grow in any leftover food. Spoon out the amount you feel your baby will eat, mark down the date the jar was opened to assure freshness, and refrigerate the leftovers.

• Store your baby food jar selections on a tiered lazy-susan type tray. No jars will be hidden and forgotten in the back of a cupboard and you'll save space since they're stacked.

• Use an infant's food grinder to puree small amounts. Some of the food from the family meal can be ground up for the baby's meal. For larger quantity preparation, a blender or food processor is better.

• Most "make your own baby food" cookbooks suggest that you freeze your pureed food in ice cube trays. When it's frozen, place your food cubes in plastic freezer bags, label and date them, and store them in the freezer. Thaw whatever you need for the next convenient meal.

• This same idea can be used with commercial baby food. Spoon the baby food from the jar into the ice cube tray. You'll have just the right serving size and no waste from spoiled uneaten food.

• Food cubes are easy to take along if you're going out. Grab a vegetable and a meat cube from the freezer, place them in containers, and by the time you reach your destination, they should be thawed and ready.

• To make nutritious cereal for your baby, pulverize natural brown rice in your blender or food processor. Cook this for almost ten minutes, using 4 T water to 1 T rice. Add milk and serve.

• Substitute or add mashed bananas or strained fruit to milk which will make your baby's dry cereal more palatable.

• Use a small wire wisk to mash bananas for your baby for fewer lumps.

Additional reading

Natural Baby Food Cookbook, by Margaret Kenda. (New York: Nash Publishing Corp., 1972.)

Making Your Own Baby Food, 2nd ed., rev., by Mary Turner. (New York: Workman Publishing Co., Inc., 1976.)

Feeding Themselves

Finger Foods

• Finger foods are the first step to self-feeding. Often a baby who will gag eating lumps from a spoon will take food quite well if allowed to finger feed. Try these popular finger foods:

1. Chunks of fruits like bananas or peaches, carefully peeled
2. Small meatballs
3. Chunks of non-stringy meat
4. Small pieces of cheese
5. Non-sugar-coated dry cereal
6. Diced cooked carrots, green beans, or beets
7. Cooked peas
8. Seedless grapes
9. Diced hard-boiled eggs
10. Noodles (Elbow macaroni sprinkled with butter and cheese is nice.)
11. Well-cooked rice

• Has your child progressed from finger foods to eating with a spoon? Let him or her try to use a fork, too. You may find that your child prefers to "jab" the food instead of sliding it onto the spoon.

• A salad fork is easier for a child to manage than a dinner fork.

• When baby is learning to self-feed, put two spoons in the bowl, one for baby to use; the other for you to feed baby with. You'll get more accomplished.

• Maneuvering food onto a spoon is easier if the food is in a bowl rather than on a flat plate.

• A mother of a little one who is just learning says that good practice for self-feeding is dry cereal and a spoon. Since cereals come in so many interesting shapes, baby will practice longer, and if anything spills, it's not a big clean-up.

• **Parents need an occasional meal alone. Feed the children early, put them to bed, and have a relaxing dinner together.**

Controlling Messes

• A small suction rack attached to the back of the high chair can hold the bib and a damp cloth.

• A friend from Pennsylvania suggests attaching a bowl to the high chair tray with a rubber suction disc. (One that has suction on both sides.) While the child will be free to self-feed, the parent won't have to worry about the bowl ending up on the floor.

• When purchasing a high chair, select one with a tray that has a raised edge. You'll have less food on the floor.

Hands in the air
while Mom cleans
the high chair

• To save myself the task of picking up after each meal, I place a section of newspaper under the high chair and after each meal roll up one page along with all the crumbs. There's always a clean piece of newspaper under the chair, all ready for the next meal.

• It's nice to establish the routine ot wiping little hands after meals before lifting ycur child from the high chair. To simplify: (1) Wipe your child's hands. (2) Give the command: "Hands in the air, please." (3) Wipe the tray quickly before baby gets a chance to put clean fingers in the messy tray again. (4) Wipe baby's mouth gently. (5) Ask baby to lower his or her arms around your neck for a big hug—and a kiss.

• Instead of giving your child a paper napkin that's easily crumpled or torn, one Daddy we know suggests giving your baby a damp washcloth.

27 *more* helpful hints on:

The Fussy Eater

• Give a picky eater only small portions, or let your child serve himself or herself. This way, your child will not be overwhelmed by the amount he or she must eat. (3-10 yrs.)

• For children who refuse vegetables, serve everyone else at the table the vegetable serving without comment. Your child more than likely will ask to try some of the food he or she was denied. (18 mo.-5 yrs.)

• Very few children like the heel of the bread. Don't throw it out. They'll never know if you put the sandwich filling on the outside crust and another slice on top. Hide that heel!

• Many fussy eaters do not like their foods mixed. If you have prepared a casserole for dinner, separate all the food before you give it to your child. (2-7 yrs.)

• Meat or raw vegetables are frequently shunned by small gourmets. They are hard to chew, so cut them into smaller bites or serve the vegetables cooked. (1-7 yrs.)

• Try to schedule snacks at regular times, not sooner than 1 1/2 hours before mealtime. If your child is not eating well at meals, observe his or her snacking pattern for a few days. (1-10 yrs.)

• If you do give snacks, make sure that they are nutritious. (See the section on "Fun Foods, Naturally".)

• A mother of two fussy eaters suggests cooking in larger quantities than necessary and freezing the extra. Whenever she is having something one family member dislikes, she thaws a favorite leftover. (1-10 yrs.)

• Don't keep foods that are not nutritious around the house. They won't be a temptation for any member of the family if they aren't there. You'll save grocery money too. (2-10 yrs.)

• Make meals as attractive as possible for fussy eaters. For instance, arrange string beans in a flower design, put a face of apple slices and raisins on hot cereal. (2-10 yrs.)

• There are a number of good children's cookbooks on the market. Let them pick out recipes to make themselves. They'll learn nutrition and the joys of cooking good food. (3-10 yrs.)

• Your older child can plant and care for a garden. He or she will surely be interested in tasting all the produce that was grown. (7-10 yrs.)

Ways to Stimulate Interest in Food

Some successful approaches from many parents of many fussy eaters:

• Pack your child's lunch in a lunchbox. (18 mo.-4 yrs.)

• An independent child can be provided with a jar of peanut butter and a squeeze bottle filled with jelly, a neat way of handling a favorite lunch. (2-6 yrs.)

• Your child can help you in the preparation of some soup. He or she may try those "hated" vegetables when he or she does the chopping. (2-10 yrs.)

• Another fun soup to make together is alphabet soup. (2-10 yrs.)

• Plan a smorgasbord for lunch. Put out cheese, peanut butter, cold cuts, tuna, or egg salad. Let your child create a lunch. (3-10 yrs.)

• Place the food on a new placemat—one with a picture of your child's favorite super hero or Sesame Street character. Forget the plate and let him or her eat on the placemat. (2-7 yrs.)

• Or have your child create a placemat. See instructions in the "Inside Fun" section. (3-10 yrs.)

• Serve your child a "mystery lunch." Cover his or her eyes and let your child select a piece of food and guess what it is. (2-6 yrs.)

• Pack a nibble bag. Put his or her name on a brown paper bag and fill it with dry cereal, raisins, and peanuts mixed together. Your child will enjoy the nutritious snack. (2-8 yrs.)

• Special occasion paper plates go on sale after the holiday. Stock up and serve food on decorative plates for special meals, a picnic, or a surprise party. (2-10 yrs.)

• My Mom always had a supply of "different" utensils on hand to interest her fussy eaters. She had pickle forks, serving forks, melon or grapefruit spoons, small gravy ladles for soups, and an assortment of plastic silverware. (3-10 yrs.)

• Get an old blanket and let your child have a picnic in your back yard. He or she may even want to invite some friends to the party. (2-10 yrs.)

• You can invite a puppet, a doll, or a stuffed animal friend to lunch, too. (2-8 yrs.)

• Just for fun, place a frisbee for support under a paper plate.

• Use the recipes in the "Fun Foods, Naturally" section.

54 *more* helpful hints on:

Fun Foods, Naturally

Kids love to cook. Let them help in the preparation, and they'll be more interested in the meal.

Children's Cooking Rules

1. Wash hands carefully.

2. Put on your special apron.

3. Be familiar with the recipe before you begin. (You don't want to be searching for equipment or running next door to borrow ingredients.)

4. Carefully measure out the ingredients. (Your cooking supervisor might want to give you some lessons on fractions while you measure halves and quarters and eighths.)

5. Tell your cooking partner not to worry about the flour, sugar, and milk that don't make it into the bowl.

6. Get out your hand beater and mix everything up.

7. A hint for your cooking supervisor is: Place the bowl in the sink before beating. The sides of the sink will catch some of the flying mixture.

8. Insist that you make a child-size portion along with the regular size. Chefs insist on tasting creations as soon as they come out of the oven.

9. Be sure to clean up. Set the timer and see if you can tidy up the kitchen before it's time for the food to come out of the oven. (3-10 yrs.)

The following recipes are child-tested favorites suggested by family and friends.

Breakfast and Lunch

• Children always like waffles or pancakes. Instead of spreading syrup on them, place honey in a squeeze bottle—the kind used for ketchup or mustard—for a no-mess kid-prepared meal.

• Freeze large numbers of waffles and pancakes in advance and heat them in a toaster (set on light, run through twice) or toaster oven.

• An older child can have fun making his or her own toasted sandwich in the waffle iron.

• Children can easily separate egg yolks from whites if they are cracked into their hands. The white will run through the fingers and the yolks remain in the palms.

• After scrambling eggs, your child can decorate them with pieces of cheese. Make a face, and sprinkle grated cheese around for hair.

• Another fun way to eat an egg is to make a "frog in a hole." Either fry an egg sunny side up or poach it and place it on a plate. Take a slice of bread, tear or cut a hole in the center with a cookie cutter, and place the bread over the egg, with the yolk peeking out of the hole in the bread. Cover the yolk with the circle and let your child try to find the "frog in the hole."

• It doesn't have to be Easter to decorate eggs. (You and your child can draw faces on hard-boiled eggs. Then, pick out favorites to eat!

• Add food coloring to oatmeal or cream of wheat. It looks like a new meal.

• Toast slices of bread, spread with butter, sprinkle coconut on top, and enjoy.

• Soak dried fruits or simmer until soft, then blend and use as a spread for toast.

• To perk up interest in a sandwich, have your child use metal cookie cutters to cut the bread into different shapes. (Thin-sliced bread works best.) Your child will really enjoy heart and half moon sandwiches.

• As a variation, use the cookie cutter on the filling. Cut out a piece of cheese and place it on a piece of whole wheat bread.

Her personalized snack:

chex cereals
oat "o" cereal
peanuts
raisins
toasted coconut
sunflower seeds
carob chips
chopped dates
pretzels
etc. etc.
etc.
etc. etc.

• The next time you bake bread, have your child roll some of the dough around a hot dog (nitrite-free) or a piece of cheese. Bake the bread according to the recipe and serve your child a roll with a hidden surprise.

• *A Pickle Dog:* Slice a hot dog in half, place cheese and a pickle in the middle, and place it under the broiler.

• *Two-way Cookie:* A yummy afternoon project kids can do themselves. Melt one stick of margarine or butter (your job) and mix with 3 cups of oatmeal. Add 2/3 cup honey, 3 tablespoons cocoa (the unsweetened kind), 1 cup powdered milk, 1/2 teaspoon salt, 2 teaspoons vanilla, 1/2 cup peanut butter, 1/2 cup raisins and mix thoroughly. Form into balls. Now, if you can extricate this from the kids, either bake the balls on a greased cookie sheet at 350°F. for 10 to 12 minutes, or chill them in the refrigerator for an hour or so. The dough may also be eaten as is—a fact your children will quickly discover—but it tastes a little better after chilling or cooking. This is a very sweet cookie; you may want to reduce the honey to about 1/2 cup.

• *Instant Pizza:* Split a whole wheat English muffin in half; put some spaghetti sauce on it; sprinkle some parmesan cheese over it; and place it under the broiler.

• Plan a cook-out with children and make child-size hamburgers. Use your round cookie cutter to make the shape. They're easy to eat, and just big enough so there's no waste.

• *Flower Salad:* A mound of cottage cheese surrounded by pineapple chunk "petals" (or any other fruit your child would like to add).

Peanut Butter and Banana

• *Homemade Peanut Butter:* 3 cups roasted peanuts, 3 T peanut oil. Blend until smooth; add salt. For crunchy style, add chopped nuts by hand. Other additions: honey, sesame seeds, orange bits.

• *Peanut Butter Gook:* Mix together: 2 T peanut butter, 2 teaspoons honey, 1 teaspoon raisins, 1 teaspoon wheat germ, 1 teaspoon sunflower seeds, 1 teaspoon granola. Spread on graham crackers.

• Make a graham cracker sandwich by placing peanut butter between two crackers.

• Slice a banana in half lengthwise; spread peanut butter on one half of it; and place the other half on top for a peanut butter banana sandwich.

Jessica's Stew:
1 cup milk
1 slice bread,
Child tears
bread, adds
to milk.

(handed down by her grandfather.)

• Or slice the bananas width-wise and make circles. These round sandwiches are easier to manage.

• *Ants on a Log:* Fill celery with cream cheese or peanut butter and have your child "dot" the filling with raisins. (Be careful of the strings on celery, they're hard to chew.)

• Place bananas on popsicle sticks. They are easier to handle and fun to eat.

• *Banana Pops:* Peel bananas, cut in half crosswise. Insert a stick and freeze. They can then be coated with this mixture: 6 oz. melted carob bits, with 4 cups peanut butter. Cool frosting slightly before frosting fruit. Wrap each in aluminum foil and return to freezer. Makes enough for 6 bananas.

• *Nutty Frozen Bananas:* 6 bananas, 1/2 can (3 oz.) frozen orange juice concentrate, 3/4 cup finely chopped almonds. Peel bananas, place on a square of foil or waxed paper on a cookie sheet, and coat each with 1 T orange juice. Chill in freezer about 15 minutes. Roll each in 2 T nuts, pressing to coat. Set in freezer to firm.

• *More Banana:* Roll frozen banana halves in 1 T melted crunchy peanut butter, then in 1 T toasted wheat germ

• *Peanut Butter Banana Pops:* 1 cup milk, 1 ripe banana cut into chunks, 1/2 cup creamy peanut butter, then 1/2 teaspoon vanilla. Blend, pour into popsicle molds.

• *Filled Apples:* Cut an apple into quarters and remove the core. Fill each apple with peanut butter or cream cheese.

• *Anything Mix:* Mix together granola, honey, peanut butter, coconut, raisins, and anything else your child can think of, let it sit about 15 minutes, and roll into small balls. Other additions could be: chopped nuts, sunflower seeds, dates, cereal, sesame seeds.

• For those of you with kids who don't like bananas, substitute your favorite fruit such as apples or pears. (Avoid substitutions with the recipes that require freezing.)

Fruits and Vegetables
Kids are marvelous salad makers.

• Have your child sprout beans to add to a salad. To sprout, soak 1/4 cup of lentils, chick-peas, mung beans, alfalfa, or soybeans overnight in a bowl of lukewarm water. Then place the soaked seeds into a quart jar, cover the top of the jar with cheesecloth or nylon mesh and secure tightly. Place the jar on its side, so that seeds form a thin layer, in a dark place where it is warm and humid. At least three times a day, rinse the sprouts by pouring lukewarm water into the jar, swirling around and pouring out the excess. Sprouts will develop in three to five days. Store in covered containers in the refrigerator. They will keep up to a week. Use the whole sprouted seed.

• A good way to get your child to eat fruits and vegetables is to let him or her make a people salad. Half a pear or a pineapple slice can make a body; celery or carrot sticks for arms and legs; a banana-slice head; raisin eyes; cheese hair; and lettuce or spinach clothes. Let your child create a person and then eat him up.

• *Caterpillars:* Peeled and thinly sliced carrots, celery sticks, cream cheese, raisins, walnuts, sliced black olives. Place a piece of carrot and a celery stick on each child's plate. Cover with cream cheese. Place other items alongside, and let kids decorate.

• *Flagpole Salad:* Arrange several different fruit slices on a plate. Slice a banana in half and stand it on end.

• *Candlelight Salad:* Half a banana inserted in a pineapple ring. A maraschino cherry on top can be the flame, with mayonnaise dribbling down as wax.

• *Orange Surprise:* Peel an orange and separate each section. Place these slices in a circle on a lettuce leaf and put a scoop of yogurt in the middle. Dip each slice of orange into the yogurt before eating.

• *Johnny Appleseed Sundae:* Place 1/4 cup applesauce in the bottom of a bowl; add 1 cup of plain or vanilla yogurt; add another 1/4 cup applesauce on top; and sprinkle with wheat germ, honey, and cinnamon.

• Dip seedless grapes into egg whites, sprinkle them with date sugar, and freeze.

• Use unflavored gelatin with your child's favorite sugar-free juice to make a more nutritious jello. Add some chunks of fruit to the mixture for a wiggly dessert with hidden surprises.

• *Apple Tea:* Save peelings and cores left over after making applesauce or an apple dessert, and simmer one to two hours. You may add honey. Strain juice into a teapot, sieve the pulp to get it all. Nice with a cinnamon stick.

• Make a fruit salad, but don't add sugar to make it sweet. As a substitute for sugar, pour fruit juice, sprinkle cinnamon, or add honey. You will have a naturally sweet and extra juicy fruit salad.

• Dilute the fruit juices you give to your children. This is not only economical, but cuts down on the high natural sugar content they contain.

• *Pumpkinitos:* Melt together: 1 1/2 T butter, 1 T salt, dash Worcestershire sauce. Stir in the seeds of a large pumpkin and bake at 250°F. for about 2 hours.

Something Cold

• *Fruit Milk Shake:* 1/3 cup frozen orange or grape juice concentrate, 1/2 cup powdered milk, 3/4 cup water, 1/2 cup ice cubes or crushed ice, 1 T peanut butter (optional). Combine in blender. One generous serving. You can use other juices instead of water.

• *Strawberry Smoothie:* 1 banana, 1 package frozen strawberries, 1 quart milk. Combine everything in a blender.

• Turn ordinary fruit juice into soda by adding one part juice to three parts club soda. This will make the juice fizz just like that sugar-filled beverage you do not want your child to have.

• Make ice cubes from fruit juice and place a real piece of fruit in the center. Drop this into your "fruit juice soda."

• Freeze left over canned fruit juices into popsicles. Or blend a can of any fruit with juice, pour into molds, and freeze.

• To make orange juice yogurt popsicles, mix equal parts of orange juice and plain yogurt and freeze in popsicle molds.

• *Clown Ice Cream Cone:* Make a face on a scoop of ice cream with nuts or raisins, then place the upside-down ice cream cone on top.

• *Nutwiches:* Mix softened ice cream with peanut butter and honey, spread between graham crackers, and freeze.

For more recipes

Creative Food Experiences for Children, rev. ed., Center for Science in the Public Interest. (Washington, D.C., 1980.) (4-10 yrs.)

Kids Are Natural Cooks, by Parents' Nursery School. (Calif.: Houghton Mifflin Co., 1971.) (3-7 years.)

Kids' Kitchen Takeover, by Sara Bonnett Stein. (New York: Workman Publishing Co., Inc., 1975.) (7-10 yrs.)

How to Help Your Child Eat Right, by Antoinette Kuzmanich Hatfield; Peggy Smelton Stanton. (Washington, D.C.: Acropolis Books, Ltd., 1978.) (1-10 yrs.)

33 *more* helpful hints on:

Kids' Rooms

Decorating

• Several parents suggested using indoor/outdoor carpeting in your child's room. It is warm; there's no chance of slipping on a throw rug; and it's easy to keep clean. (NB-10 yrs.)

• Track lighting is a good investment. No room will be taken up by a lamp and there is no chance of something being knocked over. (NB-10 yrs.)

• Cover the walls with washable wallpaper to save on clean-ups. (NB-10 yrs.)

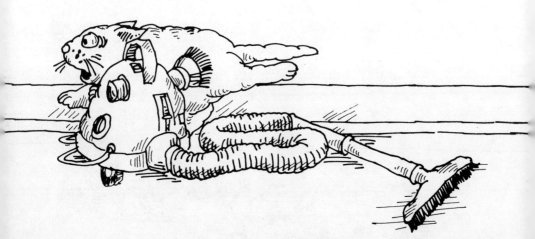

• Hang up a clothesline in your child's bedroom. Display art-work with clothespins. (2-10 yrs.)

• Put a piece of fishnet on your child's wall. Arrange and rearrange artwork using clothespins to clip everything onto the net. (2-10 yrs.)

• A piece of slate for drawing or for making notes is a good addition. You may want to scribble a note on the slate sometimes that says, "Pick up the toys in this room," for your older child. (2-10 yrs.)

• Posters and pictures are fun to have on the walls and ceiling, too. (NB-10 yrs.)

• You can get posters from stationery stores, bookstores, travel agencies, embassies, and from publishers of children's books. (NB-10 yrs.)

• My son enjoys stick-ons that glow in the dark to put on the ceiling or walls. (NB-10 yrs.)

• When your child has outgrown the crib, remove one side and the hardware; cover the mattress with a bright print; add some colored pillows; and have a child-sized settee which can double as a spare bed when friends sleep over. (3-10 yrs.)

• Bunk beds, loft beds, or a trundle bed save space. Some single beds come with drawers underneath. Make your own storage space by placing two square drawers under your child's bed. (3-10 yrs.)

• School furniture is very well made. Buy used furniture from your school, or for new furniture, look in the "Yellow Pages" under "School Equipment." (2-10 yrs.)

• For a shared room, a parent suggests using a screen as a room divider to create a secret place for your child. (NB-10 yrs.) Or build a bookcase room divider for privacy in a room for two. (NB-10 yrs.)

• A bedroom should be your children's domain. Let them help you decorate it, giving them plenty of shelf space for their private collections and treasures, and a bulletin board to pin up work and mementos. (5-10 yrs.)

• A plant in a child's bedroom helps humidify the air in winter. Let your child learn to water and care for it, to teach him or her to care for living things. The child can help you choose the plant, but read the instructions on care and necessary light so that the plant will prosper. (5-10 yrs.)

• Decorate plain white window shades by letting your child paint his own picture on each one. You can help him or her choose colors that will go with the room. (5-10 yrs.)

• Have a large piece of glass cut to fit the top of his or her desk or dresser. Treasured pictures, photos, and other precious pieces of paper can be preserved under glass. (5-10 yrs.)

• Colorful sheets on a bed can really change the look of a room. If your child likes change, let him help you choose two very different sets of sheets. When you (or the child) change the sheets, you'll change the look of the room. You can make a quick cover for a quilt by sewing two sheets together on three sides and leaving the fourth side open for easy washing. (6-10 yrs.)

• Let your child paint a picture on one wall of the room. Start out with a drawing, decide on the colors, and paint with bright acrylic paints that can be covered with either oil or acrylic paints if the child wants a change or you want to sell the house or apartment. (6-10 yrs.)

Extra Space

• Plastic stick-on hooks are a wonderful way to get extra storage in your child's room. Make sure though that you hang them higher than your child's head to prevent injury. (NB-10 yrs.)

• Old metal lockers painted bright colors offer inexpensive storage for toys or clothing. Make sure you anchor them well. (NB-10 yrs.)

• Paint mailboxes brightly and attach them to the wall. They provide handy storage space for special papers and small items. (3-10 yrs.)

• Purchase metal shelves that slip over the door for extra storage. (NB-10 yrs.)

• Hang a shoe bag in your child's room. Use it to store hats, mittens, ribbons, etc., as well as shoes. (NB-10 yrs.)

• Garment bags with shelves provide extra space for clothing or toys. (NB-10 yrs.)

• You'll have lots of storage space for hats, belts, and jackets if you cover the inside of the closet door with pegboard and add hooks. (NB-10 yrs.)

Try pegboard to tidy a doll collection.

• We gain some extra closet space by hanging a wooden mug rack on the inside of the closet for coats and jackets.

• Paint a drying rack a bright color and use it as an open closet. There's room for many shirts and blouses on hangers. A clothesline can also be used. (NB-10 yrs.)

• Build temporary shelves in the lower half of the closet.

- To store records, turn a milk crate on its side, place the records inside and the record player on top. (3-10 yrs.)

- Hang a bicycle basket over the edge of your child's bed to store pajamas. (4-10 yrs.)

- Use an old trunk or decorated foot locker for extra storage. If it has no compartments, make sections for sweaters, socks, and other clothing items. (NB-10 yrs.)

- Old milk and orange crates make attractive, convenient places to store toys, books, or clothing. Paint them different colors, turn them on their sides, or stack them.

For more information

Children's Rooms, by Ellen Levine. (New York: Bobbs-Merrill Co., Inc., 1975.)

Sunset Ideas for Children's Rooms and Play Yards, by Sunset. (Menlo Park, Calif.: Lane, 1980.)

Children's Spaces: 50 Architects and Designers Create Environments for the Young, by M. and Norman McGrath. (New York: Morrow, William & Co., Inc., 1978.)

72 *more* helpful hints on:

Bumps, Bangs, Moans and Groans

Minor Injuries

• Things to have on hand for illness or emergencies:

A first-aid chart and a first-aid book (Be sure to read through beforehand.)

Syrup of Ipecac (for accidental poisoning, but call the Poison Control Center *before* administering, *please*. Certain poisons should *not* be treated with Ipecac.)

Band aids

Sterile gauze pads

Adhesive tape

Antiseptic and antiseptic cream (Hydrogen peroxide is an excellent antiseptic.)

Cotton swabs

Cotton balls

Tongue depressors and a small purse-size flashlight for looking down throats

Children's aspirin and acetaminophen

Cough medicine

Decongestant syrup

Vaseline

Calamine lotion (without antihistamine)
Anesthetic ointment
Rectal thermometer and Clini-temp heat sensitive tape thermometer
Humidifier
Heating pad
Tweezers

• An excellent first-aid handbook is *A Sigh of Relief* by Martin I. Green. (New York: Bantam Books, Inc., 1977.) It contains simple illustrated instructions to cover every childhood injury and illness. For fast reference, the back of the book jacket has a notched alphabetical listing of illnesses and injuries which the parent can use to flip easily and quickly to the correct page.

• For a child with a specific medical problem, invest in a Medic Alert bracelet or necklace. When your child needs medical attention this will provide vital information. Write to:

> Medic Alert Foundation International
> Turlock, CA 95380

• Paint faces on band aids to help minimize the ouch, but be careful not to cover the airholes.

• An excellent tip from a practical nurse: For ouchless adhesive tape removal, rub a cotton ball saturated with baby oil over the tape before you remove it.

• Ice helps keep down the swelling on a split lip. Freeze some water in a popsicle mold for just such an emergency. It's more fun to suck on a popsicle than to hold an ice cube on your lip.

• I always keep a wet sponge in the freezer for quick application to pinches, burns, and bruises. This is better than an ice bag because it is flexible and takes the shape of the injured area. One drawback is that it loses heat quickly. Remember: Cold water or ice should be applied initially to pinches, burns, or bruises.

• Getting out a splinter hurts! An often-recommended method to ease the pain is to deaden the area with an ice cube beforehand.

• Grow an aloe plant in your kitchen window. If a finger is

burned, quickly open a leaf and hold the goo on the burn. You can also purchase aloe cream as I do, if you don't have a green thumb. (Aloe hasn't been recommended officially by doctors; ingested, it is a carthartic; non-officially, it is used for a wide variety of skin problems.)

- Vanilla relieves the pain of a burned tongue.

- Vitamin C is very good for the common cold.

- Kathleen, a mother in Bethesda, suggests keeping a stack of red napkins handy. If your child gets hurt, use the wet red napkin to stop the blood. It's not as noticeable.

- Make sure your child keeps that injured finger or hand soaking in Epsom salts. Put several small toys in the water to keep him or her amused and soaking.

- This same idea can be used to keep a burned finger soaking in a bowl of ice water. Lori, a four-year-old, preferred playing in a bowl of ice water to holding ice on her injured finger. (Specifics: bruises, strained muscles, or sprains should be put in ice first, then apply heat. Dirty cuts should be cleaned in warm water and antiseptic.)

- Last year, my son's friend, Tod, had his thumb smashed in a car door. To protect his finger from bumps his mother placed a roller-type plastic hair roller over the finger after bandaging. (Tape it securely at the base, but leave the top open for ventilation.)

- *Home remedy for insect bits:* Apply a paste of baking soda and water; use face soap; or put ice to numb it. Dilute household ammonia for stings; a paste of meat tenderizer may be used for bee or wasp stings.

- Scrape out a stinger from a wasp or bee bite with a scraping motion of your fingernail. Do not pull it out. Consult your physician promptly if there is any reaction. Symptoms are: Hives, generalized rash, pallor, weakness, nausea, vomiting, "tightness in the chest, nose, or throat," collapse, or swelling of the entire limb.

- A mother of a frequent earache-sufferer recommends a heating pad or a hot water bottle wrapped in a towel to ease the pain. (Children with persistent earaches should see a pediatrician.)

- Bill, a friend in Virginia, offers this "100% effective cure for the hiccups": Place a finger in each of your child's ears while he or she drinks a full glass of water. (This works for moms and dads, too.)

- *Poison ivy pack:* Use calamine lotion—not the kind mixed with "antihistamine". You may use cool compresses or a baking powder solution to relieve the itching. Topical steroids may be used for slightly more severe cases.

• Head injuries bleed a lot since the head is a highly vascular area. Don't panic because of the amount of blood. Apply pressure with a gauze pad or clean handkerchief.

• Calm reassurance (for both parent and child) will make the injury less traumatic.

Comfort for the Sick
Care

• Stuffy noses at night and naptime keep your little one from getting the rest he or she needs and wants. I've found that a pillow placed under the mattress elevates the head and helps my child to breathe easier. A vaporizer makes a big difference, too. Be sure to start the vaporizer before rest time so the air in the room will be moist and ready when your child is. A cold water vaporizer is best to use because it's safer—no burned fingers. (NB-10 yrs.)

• Get a good look at that sore throat by having your child pant like a dog while you shine a purse-size flashlight down the throat. (2-10 yrs.)

• A lollipop is a gag-free tongue depressor.

• Most children protest loudly when it is time to take their temperature. Before you insert the rectal thermometer, lay your child across your lap, gently pat him or her on the back or rock your child on your knees. Next, as he or she is resting across your legs, get him or her interested in a favorite book or toy. This helps distract your child while you take the temperature. For easy application, put a little lubricating jelly on the end of the rectal thermometer before you insert it. (NB-1 yr.)

• For an older child, an armpit (axilla) temperature is more acceptable and less likely to be protested. (1-6 yrs.)

• Before talking to the doctor, be prepared. *Write* down all symptoms, temperature, and any questions you have. Have a pencil and paper with you to note any instructions the doctor gives.

• If your child is having trouble keeping food down, and your p.j. supply is getting low, a man's shirt can be used instead.

• Keep a wastebasket or basin nearby in case your child can't make it to the bathroom. Line it with plastic and put newspapers underneath to save on clean-up.

• Attach a bag to the bed with a spring-type clothespin to store sick-bed equipment or trash. (3-10 yrs.)

• Give your child a bell to ring when he or she needs you. Don't be surprised if your child cries "wolf" a few times just to test it out the way mine did after his tonsillectomy. (3-10 yrs.)

• Sometimes requests for a drink are really requests for attention. Spend some time with your lonely child. After you visit though, leave a thermos of juice. The juice will stay cold, and you'll save some trips up and down stairs. (3-10 yrs.)

Medications
• *Never* give medications in the dark.

• Ask your doctor to prescribe a generic drug. It will save you money.

• Make medicine-taking time performance time. We always assemble the whole family for the event with instructions for everyone to clap and hoot after the swallow. Your child will love the applause and will forget about putting up a fuss. (18 mo.-4 yrs.)

• If applause doesn't work, bribery should. Have a treat to offer after the medicine is "all gone." (18 mo.-10 yrs.)

• Measure out the correct dosage of medicine and then use the dropper from a liquid vitamin bottle to squirt the medicine into the child's mouth. Make sure you aim the dropper to the side of the mouth, not directly down the throat. (NB-2 yrs.) A "Flexidose" spoon from the drugstore ensures an accurate dosage.

• Set an alarm clock to remind you when it is time to give your child medicine.

• Don't trust your memory when giving medications! A friend suggests keeping notes on a chalkboard as to when and what was given. This is essential if you're giving more than one medication.

• Juice also disguises medicine, but be sure to use a juice that your child doesn't usually drink. Otherwise, he or she will instantly recognize the different taste the medicine makes. (1-4 yrs.)

• Taste a bit of the medicine before you give it to your child. Tell him or her if it is going to taste bad. (4-10 yrs.)

• An often recommended medicine disguise is to dissolve or mash baby aspirin and mix it with applesauce or honey. (NB-2 yrs.) (Caution: Do not give honey to a child under the age of one). To mash a baby aspirin, put it in a spoon and mash it with the back of another spoon.

• Let your child suck on an ice cube or popsicle before he or she takes some bad-tasting medicine. This will deaden the tastebuds. (18 mo.-10 yrs.)

• Warm up ear drops by putting the container under hot water. Test carefully before using. (NB-10 yrs.)

• It's scary for your child to see an eye dropper coming head on! Have your child close his or her eyes while tilting the head back. Put a drop in the inner corner of each eye. When your child's eyes open, the drops will roll right in. (NB-10 yrs.)

Keeping Occupied
• Ways to make the Time Pass Quickly

1. New library books
2. Puzzles
3. Activity books with mazes and hidden pictures
4. Stacking toys or interlocking blocks
5. Beads to string
6. Picture dominoes, or dominoes
7. Musical instruments
8. Doctor kits
9. Flannel board
10. Magic slate
11. Viewmaster slides

• For a less lonely dinner, family members can take turns having meals in the same room with the bedridden child.

• A friend in Silver Spring says that if your child *must* stay in bed, give him or her a stack of pennies in the morning. Tell your child that every time he or she gets out of bed you will take one penny away. (3-10 yrs.)

• Artwork is always fun, especially "germ art." Give your child a bed tray, some crayons, pencils, glue, and paper and let him or her draw a picture of the bug that caused the illness. These pictures are fun to show around and save. (3-10 yrs.)

• Weaving will help to pass the time. Provide your child with a loom like the one used for making potholders and he or she can make some gifts from the sickroom. (7-10 yrs.)

• The bedridden child can keep occupied and feel useful by decorating napkins for the family dinner. (2-8 yrs.)

• Make an activity tray by cutting off the sides of a cardboard box to a height of 3" on three sides and 1" on the side facing the patient.

• Bed trays, or the snap-off top of a snack tray, make good work tables, too.

• Your child will probably miss seeing friends. Let him or her call them on the phone and hear what is happening. (3-10 yrs.)

• One of the most-often recommended ways to make the time pass quickly is a tape recorder. It provides hours of entertainment. Use the tape recorder for making up stories, singing, then make a tape to send to friends at school. (3-10 yrs.)

• A strong direct light and pair of hands can amuse a sick child or a grouchy one. Think back to your childhood and use your imagination to create shadows. We will illustrate a few to get you started. (18 mo.-10 yrs.)

• When your little one has the chicken pox, dress him or her in an old shirt or sweater with extra-long sleeves. Fold them over the hands, pin them, and draw puppet faces on them. Scratching will be forgotten as the child plays with the "puppets." (18 mo.-3 yrs.)

• For more sick-room entertainments, see the "Arts, Crafts and Activities" section.

For more ideas on how to pass the time

Strings on Your Fingers—How to Make String Figures, by Harry Helfman. (New York: Morrow, William & Co., Inc., 1965.) (6-10 yrs.)

It's Magic, by Robert Lopshire. (New York: MacMillan Publishing Co., Inc., 1969.) (preschool-8 yrs.)

New Complete Hoyle, the Official Rules of All Popular Games of Skill and Chance, by Albert Morehead. (New York: New American Library, 1963.) (6-10 yrs.)

A Visit to the Doctor

• Buy a child's doctor kit. Explain what all the instruments are and let your child play doctor with you or with a doll. Your child will be much more comfortable and confident when it's time for a visit.

• Find out what is going to happen to your child at the next visit. Prepare for the visit by answering questions honestly, and if your child asks if the doctor will give him or her a shot, don't lie.

• Help your child get over anxieties about a shot by comparing it to a pinch. Have a pinching session. Exchange pinches with your child; from then on refer to a shot as getting a pinch. It's not so scary.

• While you are waiting for the doctor, color the paper on the examining table to take your child's mind off the visit. A pad of paper works just as well as taking along a book or toy.

- Take along your child's favorite blanket or stuffed animal.

- Hold your young child as much as possible during the exam.

For more comfort, read

My Friend the Doctor, by Jane Werner Watson, Robert E. Switzer, M.D., and Jay Cotter Hirschberg, M.D. (Golden Press, New York: Western Publishing Co., Inc., 1972.) (3-6 yrs.)

How the Doctor Knows You're Fine, by Vicki Cobb. (New York: Lippincott, J.B., Co., 1973.) (5-10 yrs.)

My Doctor, by Harlow Rockwell. (New York: MacMillan Publishing Co., Inc., 1973.) (2-5 yrs.)

Teething

- Something cold always feels good on your child's gums. Teething rings that can be refrigerated or frozen work very well. Have several in the refrigerator so when one thaws out and warms up, you'll have a replacement ready.

- Before your child's teeth come in, raw fruits and vegetables—carrots, apples, or frozen seedless orange slices—make good teethers because they're hard and cold. Once your child gets the first tooth though, don't use these. He or she may bite off a piece of fruit or vegetable and choke on it.

- A cold wet tea towel makes a good teether. Children like to pull the rough cloth across their gums.

- To help numb those sore gums, wrap an ice cube in a handkerchief and have your child suck on this—with Mom or Dad in attendance that is.

- Tie a round frozen bagel on to a string. It's nice and hard and will last a while. If the bagel becomes crumbly, take it away. Baby may choke. Caution: Be careful of the length of the string.

- Sucking increases the blood supply to baby's already sore and swollen gums and aggravates the situation. Try enlarging the hole in the nipple of baby's bottle or offering a cup to cut down on the sucking.

• Drooling accompanies teething in some babies. Let your child wear a bib around all day to absorb the drips.

• A hard heel of bread feels good to teething gums, but please don't buy teething biscuits. Not only do they contain sugar, but they make an incredibly sticky, gooey mess.

90 *more* helpful hints on:

Safety

Precautions

• Contact the American Red Cross and take a First Aid Course.

• Make sure that you learn the Heimlich Method for victims of choking.

• Take a Cardio-Pulmonary Resusitation Course (CPR) if you find one offered. They cost little in time or money.

• Purchase a fire extinguisher for your home.

• Install smoke alarms.

• Get Mr. Yuk stickers for all your poisons. Make sure your child is familiar with the stickers, and that he or she understands their meaning. These stickers are warnings that should be used in addition to keeping all poisonous substances under lock and key or in cupboards secured with childsafe locks.

• To obtain one dozen Mr. Yuk stickers and information on teaching your children about poison prevention, send $1.00 to:

National Poison Center Network
125 DeSoto Street
Pittsburgh, PA 15213

• **Mr. Yuk,** *the poison warning symbol of the National Poison Center Network, Children's Hospital of Pittsburgh.*

• Put Mr. Yuk stickers on products like these:

Acids	Drain cleaners	Oven cleaner
Aerosols	Drugs	Paint
Ammonia	Epoxy glue	Paint thinner
Antiseptics	Eye make-up	Permanent wave solution
Aspirin	Furniture polish	Pesticides
Bathroom bowl cleaner	Garden sprays	Petroleum distillates
Benzene	Gun cleaners	Pine oil
Bubble bath	Hair dyes	Rodenticides
Carbon tetrachloride	Herbicides	Shaving lotion
Cigarettes	Insecticides	Silver polish
Cleaning fluids	Iodine	Strychnine
Clinitest tablets	Kerosene	Turpentine
Cologne	Mace (chemical)	Typewriter cleaner
Copper & brass cleaners	Model cement	Vitamins
Corn & wart remover	Nail polish	Window wash solvent
Dandruff shampoo	Nail polish remover	
Dishwasher detergents	Narcotics	

First Aid For Plant Exposures

Swallowed:
1. Remove any remaining plant material from mouth.
2. Rinse mouth with water.
3. If signs of burns or irritations, give milk.
4. Bring plant and patient to phone if possible.
5. Call the local Poison Control Center immediately.

Eye contamination:
1. Flush eye with water immediately for at least fifteen minutes. (Hold head under the faucet as if washing hair. (DO NOT USE AN EYE CUP.)
2. Call the local Poison Control Center as soon as eye is thoroughly rinsed.

Skin Contamination:
1. Rinse skin well with soapy water.
2. **DO NOT apply any cream, lotion, ointment, etc.**
3. Call the local Poison Control Center as soon as possible.

50 Common Harmful Plants

Remember—these plants are not the ONLY plants that could be harmful to you and your family. If you have questions about any plants, cultivated and wild, please call your Poison Center for prompt, professional advice.

CULTIVATED HOUSE AND GARDEN PLANTS	TOXIC PARTS	SYMPTOMS PRODUCED
1. **Caladium** *Fancy-leaf caladium*	All parts (Toxic substance: Calcium oxalate crystals)	Intense irritation to mucous membranes producing swelling of tongue, lips and palate
2. **Colocasia** *Elephant ear, Dasheen*	Same as above	Same as above
3. **Dieffenbachia** *Dumb cane, Elephant ear*	Same as above	Same as above
4. **Monstera** *Swiss-cheese plant, Ceriman*	Same as above	Same as above
5. **Philodendron** *Elephant ear*	Same as above	Same as above

Arum family (bracketing items 1–5)

CULTIVATED HOUSE AND GARDEN PLANTS	TOXIC PARTS	SYMPTOMS PRODUCED
6. **Ricinus communis** *Castor bean, Castor-oil plant Palma Christi*	Seed, if chewed; (Toxic substance: Ricin)	Burning sensation in the mouth, nausea, vomiting, abdominal pain, thirst, blurred vision, dizziness, convulsions
7. **Lantana** *Lantana*	All parts, especially the green berries (Toxic substance: Lantadene A)	Vomiting, diarrhea, weakness, ataxia, visual disturbances and lethargy
8. **Lantana** *Hens-and-Chicks*	Same as above	Same as above
9. **Lantana** *Bunchberry*	Same as above	Same as above
10. **Hedera helix** *English ivy*	All parts (Toxic substance: Hederagenin, or steroidal saponin)	Local irritation, excess salivation, nausea, vomiting, thirst, severe diarrhea, abdominal pain
11. **Digitalis** *Foxglove*	Leaves, seeds, flowers (Toxic substances: Cardio-active glycosides—digitoxin, digoxin, gitoxin and others)	Local irritation of mouth and stomach, vomiting, abdominal pain, diarrhea, cardiac disturbances
12. **Rhododendron** *Rhododendron*	All parts (Toxic substance: Andromedotoxin)	Watering of eyes and mouth, nasal discharge, loss of appetite, nausea, vomiting, abdominal pain, paralysis of the limbs and convulsions
13. **Rhododendron** *Azalea*	Same as above	Same as above
14. **Delphinium** *Larkspur, Crowfoot*	All parts, especially the seeds (Toxic substance: Delphinine)	Burning and inflammation of mouth, lips and tongue, followed by numbness; paresthesia, beginning in the extremities, progressing to entire body
15. **Delphinium**	Same as above	Same as above
16. **Hydrangea macrophylia** *Hydrangea*	Leaves and buds (Toxic substance: Cyanogenic glycoside —hydragin)	Nausea, vomiting, abdominal pain, diarrhea, difficulty breathing, muscular weakness, dizziness, stupor and convulsions

CULTIVATED HOUSE AND GARDEN PLANTS	TOXIC PARTS	SYMPTOMS PRODUCED
17. **Pyrus sylvestris** *Apple*	Seeds (Toxic substance: Cyanogenic glycoside) —hydrangin)	Nausea, vomiting, abdominal pain, diarrhea, difficulty breathing, muscular weakness, dizziness, stupor and convulsions
18. **Convallaria majalis** *Lily of the Valley*	All parts (Toxic substance: Cardioactive glyco-side—convallamaro-genin)	Local irritation of the mouth and stomach, followed by vomiting, abdominal pain, diarrhea, persistent headache and cardiac disturbances
19. **Lathyrus odoratus** *Sweet pea*	Pea or seed (Toxic substance: Beta-(gamma-L-glutamyl)-amino-propionitrile)	Slowed and weakened pulse, depressed and weakened respiration, and convulsions
20. **Ipomoea violaces** *Morning glory*	Seeds (Toxic substances: Several alkaloids that are chemically relat-ed to lysergic acid diethylamide, or LSD)	Hallucination-like states, nausea, loss of appetite, abdominal pain, explosive diarrhea, frequent urina-tion and depressed reflexes
21. **Hyacinthus orientalis** *Hyacinth*	Bulb; leaves and flowers if eaten in large quantities (Toxic substance: Unidentified)	Nausea, vomiting, abdominal pain and diarrhea
22. **Ilex** *Holly,* *Christmas holly* **Ilex vomitoria** *Yaupon holly*	Bright red berries (Toxic substance: Unidentified)	Nausea, vomiting, abdominal pain and diarrhea
23. **Iris** *Iris*	Rootstalk or rhizome (Toxic substance: Unidentified)	Nausea, vomiting, abdominal pain and diarrhea
24. **Ligustrum** *Common privet*	Leaves and berries (Toxic substance: Unidentified)	Nausea, vomiting, abdominal pain and diarrhea
25. **Ligustrum** *Waxed-leaf ligustrum*	Same as above	Same as above

CULTIVATED HOUSE AND GARDEN PLANTS	TOXIC PARTS	SYMPTOMS PRODUCED
26. **Narcissus** *Narcissus*	Bulb (Toxic substance: Unidentified)	Nausea, vomiting, abdominal pain and diarrhea
27. **Narcissus** *Daffodil*	Same as above	Same as above
28. **Narcissus** *Jonquil*	Same as above	Same as above
29. **Poinciana gilliesii** *Poinciana, Bird-of-Paradise*	Green seed pods (Toxic substance: Unidentified)	Nausea, vomiting, abdominal pain and diarrhea
30. **Wisteria** *Wisteria*	Whole pods or seeds (Toxic substances: Resin and glycoside wisterin)	Nausea, vomiting, abdominal pain and diarrhea
31. **Nerum oleander** *Oleander*	Leaves, stems and flowers (Toxic substances: Cardioactive glyco-sides—oleandroside, oleandrin and nerioside)	Local irritation to mouth and stomach, vomiting, abdominal pain, diarrhea and cardiac disturbances
32. **Taxus** *Japanese yew*	Seeds and leaves (Toxic substance: Alkaloid toxine)	Gastroenteritis and cardi-ac disturbances
33. **Prunus americana** *American plum, Wild plum*	Leaves, stems, bark and seed pits (Toxic substances: Cyanogenic glycosides)	Nausea, vomiting, abdominal pain, diarrhea, difficulty in breathing, muscular weakness, dizziness, stupor and convulsions
34. **Prunus armeniaca** *Apricot*	Leaves, stem, bark and seed pits (Toxic substances: Cyanogenic glycosides)	Nausea, vomiting, abdominal pain, diarrhea, difficulty in breathing, muscular weakness, dizziness, stupor and convulsions
35. **Prunus virginiana** *Choke cherry*	Leaves, stems, bark and seed pits (Toxic substances: Cyanogenic glycosides)	Nausea, vomiting, abdominal pain, diarrhea, difficulty in breathing, muscular weakness, stupor and convulsions

CULTIVATED HOUSE AND GARDEN PLANTS	TOXIC PARTS	SYMPTOMS PRODUCED
36. **Solanum pseudocapsicum** *Jerusalem cherry, Natal cherry*	All parts (Toxic substances: Leaves contain cardioactive substance solanocapsine; berries contain glycoalkaloid solanine and related glycoalkaloids)	Cardiac depression
37. **Daphne mezereum** *Daphne*	All parts, especially berries, bark and leaves (Toxic substance: Daphnin)	Local irritation to mouth and stomach, nausea, vomiting and diarrhea
38. **Rheum raponticum** *Rhubarb*	Leaf blade (Toxic substance: Oxalic acid)	Corrosive action on the gastrointestinal tract

WILD PLANTS	TOXIC PARTS	SYMPTOMS PRODUCED
39. **Arisaema triphyllum** *Jack-in-the-Pulpit, Indian turnip*	Leaves (Toxic substance: Calcium oxalate crystals)	Corrosive action to gastrointestinal tract, producing swelling of tongue, lips and palate
40. **Podophyllum peltatum** *Mayapple, Mandrake, Ground lemon*	Rootstalk, leaves, stems and green fruit (Toxic substance: Podophylloresin)	Abdominal pain, vomiting, diarrhea and pulse irregularities
41. **Cicuta maculata** *Water hemlock, Spotted cowbane, Poison parsnip*	Root and rootstalk (Toxic substance: (Cicutoxin)	Increased salivation, abdominal pain, nausea, vomiting, tremors, muscle spasms and convulsions
42. **Parthenocissus quinquefolia** *Virginia creeper, American ivy*	Berries and leaves (Toxic substance: Oxalic acid)	Corrosive action to gastrointestinal tract, nausea, vomiting, abdominal pain, diarrhea and headache
43. **Conium maculatum** *Poison hemlock Fool's parsley, False parsley*	All parts (Toxic substances: Lambda-coniceine, coniine, n-methyl coniine)	Gastrointestinal distress, muscular weakness, convulsions and respiratory distress

WILD PLANTS	TOXIC PARTS	SYMPTOMS PRODUCED
44. **Datura meteloides** *Moonflower, Angel's trumpet, Locoweed*	Leaves, flowers, nectar, seeds (Toxic substances: Belladonna alkaloids)	Dilated pupils, dry mouth, increased body temperature, intense thirst, confusion, delirium, hallucinations and pulse disturbances
45. **Datura stramonium** *Jimsonweed, Jamestown weed, Thorn apple, Angel's trumpet*	Same as above	Same as above
46. **Robinia pseudoacacia** *Black locust, White locust*	Young leaves, inner bark, seeds (Toxic substances: Robin and Robitin)	Nausea, vomiting and abdominal pain
47. **Phytolacca americana** *Pokeweed, Pokeroot, Poke salad, Inkberry*	All parts, especially the root, leaves and green berries (Toxic substance: Tannin)	Oral burning sensation, sore throat, nausea, vomiting and blurred vision
48. **Gelsemium sempervirens** *Yellow jessamine, Carolina jessamine*	All parts (Toxic substances: Alkaloids—gelsemine, gelsemicine)	Cardiac depression, visual disturbances, dizziness, headache and dryness of mouth
49. **Solanum dulcamara** *European bittersweet, Climbing nightshade*	Leaves and berries (Toxic substance: Solanine)	Vomiting, diarrhea, abdominal pain, drowsiness, tremors, weakness and difficulty in breathing
50. **Atropa belladonna** *Deadly nightshade*	All parts (Toxic substances: Tropane alkaloids, atropine and hyoscyamina)	Fever, visual disturbances, burning of mouth, thirst, dry skin, headache and confusion

Reprinted through the courtesy of the National Poison Center Network, Childrens Hospital of Pittsburgh, 125 Desoto Street, Pittsburgh, PA 15213 (412) 647-5600.

• Have an emergency phone list by your telephone, not only for yourself, but for your babysitter as well.

EMERGENCY PHONE LIST

Pediatrician: _____

Dentist: _____

Poison Control Center: _____

Hospital: _____

Police: _____

Fire Department:_____

Pharmacy: _____

Two neighbors to call for help: _____

Mother's work: _____

Father's work: _____

• Post a first aid instruction sheet on the inside of a kitchen cabinet or bathroom cabinet door and a Heimlich chart in the kitchen. Even if you know the method, the babysitter may not. Point it out.

• Keep a card handy with a health record of each family member. Record illnesses, medications, immunizations, allergies, accidents, and keep it in a handy place to grab in an emergency. Periodically update it.

• Before your baby begins to move about, it's time to child-proof your house. To look at it through the child's eyes, get down on your hands and knees; hope the neighbors aren't looking in the windows, and make a crawling tour of your home, slowly and carefully, room by room.

• Repeat your childproofing inspection every six months. Things that he or she could not reach a few months ago may now cause injury.

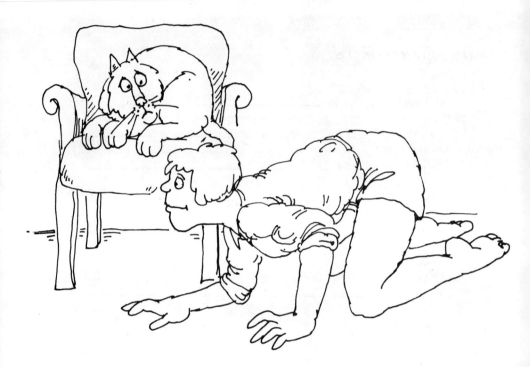

• It's a good idea for parents to have an occasional emergency drill. Sit down and talk about exactly what each of you would do in various emergencies, so that in the event that one does occur, you will be somewhat prepared to cope, and you won't waste valuable minutes running around in confusion. (3-10 yrs.)

• Children always enjoy games. Use this interest as a teaching tool. Prepare them for emergencies by having them provide solutions to unexpected situations that you create, i.e. talking to strangers, being separated from Mom and Dad in a crowd, or hearing the fire alarm go off. (3-10 yrs.)

• Begin each bedtime story with "This is a story for . . . and insert your child's name and address. When your child knows his or her name and address, add the phone number to the story. (2-7 yrs.)

For more information
Parents' Guide to Child Safety, by Vincent Fontana. (New York: Crowell, Thomas Y., Co., 1973.)

Prevention

In the Nursery

• *Never* leave baby alone for even a moment on a bed, a changing table, or any high place.

• Enjoy your baby. Cuddle your child while you feed him or her the bottle. *Never* leave a baby with a bottle propped up. Your child may spit up and inhale liquids.

• Do not place a crib near an electric outlet or a lamp.

• Windows are also dangerous spots to locate a crib. Your child may become entangled in a cord from the blind, break the glass with a toy, or decide to try to climb.

• If you have a child who enjoys rocking his crib all over the room, remove the wheels from the bed. Consider anchoring the legs to the baseboard, too.

• Slats on a crib should not be more than 2 1/2" apart. A child's head could get stuck between them.

• If your child is climbing out of the crib, don't scold. Teach him or her the right way. Put some pillows or mattresses on the floor just in case, even a stepstool can help out. Then, think about shopping for a single bed.

• *Never* hang a mirror in the crib or too near it. They shatter easily.

• Vaporizers and portable heaters are potentially dangerous. Keep them out of baby's reach.

• Check clothing for adherence to flammability requirements.

• When baby begins to sit up, avoid toys that string across the crib

• Check toys periodically for sharp edges or broken or lose parts. Either repair or discard.

• Don't let the baby chew or suck on a balloon, inflated or not. He or she may inhale part of it and block off the windpipe.

The Bathroom

• Never leave your child unattended in the bath or pool for a second. If the phone rings, ignore it. If it's important enough they'll call back.

• Keep the bathroom door closed and the toilet lid down. If your child decides to play in the toilet, he or she may lose his or her balance, fall in and not be able to push out.

• To keep your child from accidentally being locked in a room—especially the bathroom—put a piece of tape across the doorknob bolt so it won't slip into the door jamb. Or put the tape over the strikeplate.

• Lower the water temperature to 120°F. to prevent accidentally scalding your child.

• Check the temperature of bath water with your elbow before putting your child in the tub.

• Paint a red dot on the hot water faucet with red nail polish. Make sure that your child understands its meaning. Remove the dot with nail polish remover when he or she is older.

• Bathtubs are slippery! Adhesive strips or bath mats prevent slips and falls.

• Glass cups or containers don't belong in the bathroom. Use paper cups instead.

• Keep all your medical preparations locked in a metal box, out of reach. Keep the key out of reach, too. Be sure to have a spare made.

• Discard all unusable or unlabeled medicines.

The Kitchen
• Use placemats instead of tablecloths that hang over the edge of the table. A toddler can pull the tablecloth and anything on the table onto himself or herself.

• Never leave pot handles hanging over the edge of the stove. Your child may grab for the handle and spill the contents.

• Remove the knobs from the gas range when it is not in use.

• The kitchen should be off-limits when you're cooking. Put your infant in a high chair or playpen, or put a safety gate across the doorway.

• Lock up the trash. Your curious little one could get cut on an opened tin can lid, break a glass bottle, or ingest the remains of a household cleaner.

• Don't leave appliance cords dangling. When the toaster or blender are not in use, unplug them, roll up the cord, stuff it into an empty toilet paper tube, or tie it with a rubber band.

• If a glass is broken on an uncarpeted floor, use a damp paper towel for the final clean-up. All those hard-to-see glass slivers will adhere to the wet towel.

• Who ever said cleaning supplies belong under the sink? Put your canned goods there and your cleaning supplies up high, secured with childproof locks.

• Accidental poisonings occur when the substance is being used and the bottle is open. Never leave anything out if your phone rings or someone knocks at the door. After you use a poisonous substance, immediately return it to a locked cabinet.

Inside
• Do you know what one of the most dangerous things in your house is? It's the telephone. Children get into more trouble while Mom or Dad is distracted by conversation and anchored to one spot. Don't let your child out of your sight for a minute when the phone rings.

• When your child is learning to walk, there are a lot of falls and bumps. Buy guards for the sharp edges of your coffee table or tape foam rubber or cotton on the edges to prevent bad injuries.

• The addition of a light switch extender helps your child avoid dangerous climbing to reach a switch in a dark room.

• Bolt dresser, bookshelves, or any tippable furniture. Secure them to the floor with L-braces or to the wall with a hook and eye.

• Televisions, stereo speakers, and aquariums can also come tumbling down on a climber. Anchor them also or make them inaccessible.

• Keep all electrical outlets covered with child safety caps.

• Place safety guards in front of open heaters, fireplaces, and around floor furnaces and registers.

• Replace the grill on your fan with a piece of window screen. This will keep curious little fingers out.

• No place is off limits for your inquisitive toddler. Never leave cosmetics, pins, medications, or any other type of dangerous object on your dresser. Children *will* come into your room.

• Guard against lead poisoning. Children do chew on painted surfaces, so when repainting children's furniture and toys always use only lead-free paint labeled: "Conforms to USA Standard Z 661-1964."

• Discard plastic bags or place them in a locked cabinet out of reach. A child can suffocate in a very short time if he or she gets hold of a plastic bag.

• Never leave trunks, large picnic coolers, or discarded refrigerators where a child can crawl in and suffocate.

• Empty vitamin bottles with child-proof lids are good for storing dangerous sewing supplies.

Steps, Stairs, Doors, and Windows
• When baby begins to crawl, put gates at stairways and porches.

• Never park a carriage or stroller near an open stairway, driveway, or incline.

• Give your child a little practice crawling up and down stairs. Put the safety gate up a few steps instead of at the bottom.

• Small rugs pose a danger at the top of stairs. A child may slip and fall.

• To make rugs in other parts of the house slip-proof, sew a rubber canning jar ring at each corner.

• Add an extra-low handle to your screendoor so your toddler won't get off balance while stretching for a too-high handle when he or she wants to come in.

• It's hard for children to tell when a sliding glass door is closed. To prevent mishaps, put colored tape where it's easily noticed.

• Paint the bottom step of a flight of outside steps a bright or light color. Or paint the edge of each step a bright color.

• Want to let some fresh clean air into your house? Open the window from the top, not from the bottom.

• Childproof your windows with a burglar latch. These will only permit the window to open a few inches and will not spoil the appearance of your home.

Outside

• Keep your child in the yard. Place a hook and eye on the *outside* of the gate, near the ground. You will be able to reach over and unlatch it, your child can't.

• Don't let your child in the yard when the lawn mower is in use. It often throws out dangerous objects like stones, wires, or broken glass.

• Make large cardboard stop signs and place them at the end of your driveway or any place your child should not ride a tricycle.

• Attach large orange bicycle flags to your child's tricycle. Anyone backing out or coming into your driveway will know your child is there.

• A friend suggests placing a piece of adhesive tape around each wheel of a pair of roller skates to slow them down and help cut down on falls. By the time your child is proficient, the tape will be worn away and he or she can speed around the patio.

• Don't let kids play with long or sharp sticks. Running and falling while holding a stick can seriously injure a child. Keep this in mind when giving them flags, toy fishing poles, stick horses, or similar stick items.

• While playing on gym equipment, make sure your child is not wearing a long scarf, or anything around the neck that could become caught and pulled.

• Periodically check all play equipment for loose screws and sharp edges.

• Place tape on the swing where your child should place his or her hands when swinging. Your child will be able to maintain his or her balance better.

• Stain rather than paint a home-made swing. Latex paint makes the swing slippery.

• A friend suggests oulining your playpen with double faced tape to keep crawling insects from making their way inside.

In the Car

• Never go anywere in the car unless your child is restrained in a carseat.

• When a restraint is used from birth, it becomes a natural part of riding in the car for the child, and the beginning of a life-time habit of using safety belts after outgrowing the infant and toddler seats.

• Once your child outgrows his or her car seat (usually when the child weighs more than 40 lbs.), insist that your child use a safety or restraining harness.

• Once you've reached your destination, it's just as important to watch out for caught fingers. Establish a routine for keeping fingers away from the doors *and* for not running into the traffic once they're out of the car (which children are tempted to do). One example is to have them hold their arms in the air for a stretch after the ride or to give themselves a hug, as before.

• Having a slogan might help, too: Be a statue. Don't run!!!

• Set a good example. Every time you buckle up, your child learns a valuable lesson.

• Make sure you know where everyone's fingers are before you shut the car door. Have the children give themselves a hug, or ask them to put their hands in their laps. Once you've been obeyed, close the doors.

46 *more* helpful hints on:

Getting Along

Siblings

• Your first child has always been the center of attention, and will be quite upset when some of his or her exclusive time is spent with the new baby. To help with the adjustment, make your child aware of the fact that he or she is not the *only* important thing in parents' lives. Parents can do this by going out alone and leaving the child with other family members, for example. (2-10 yrs.)

• Get your child used to others doing things for him or her. Invite a relative or a babysitter over to help with meals, bathtime, or playtime. Or Mom and Dad can occasionally exchange the jobs they normally do. (There will be a lot of switching when the baby arrives.) (2-10 yrs.)

• Avoid any big changes once baby arrives. (2-10 yrs.)

• Teach your child how to care for a baby. When you are home you'll be surprised by how interested your child is in practicing what he or she has learned and what a big help your older child can be. (3-10 yrs.)

• Completely dismantle the crib well before the birth of the baby. Have your child select new furnishings and become familiar with them. When baby arrives, you may even want to repaint the crib for the second child. (3-4 yrs.)

• Select a hospital where sibling visitations are permitted. Take a tour of the hospital with your child before the baby is born. (3-10 yrs.)

• Refer to the baby as "our baby."

• When mother is at the hospital, the new baby can send gifts home to the older child. This really worked well for us. (2-10 yrs.)

• Those goodies the hospital bombards you with seem wonderful to the child at home. Send home flexible straws, small packets of food, (jelly, salt, pepper) plastic cups, etc. (2-10 yrs.)

• If possible, buy your older child a doll that is the same sex as the infant. Let him or her take out jealousy or anger on the doll, in addition to caring for the baby doll while you care for yours. (3-10 yrs.)

• Lessen the jealousy a child feels toward the new child by having him or her draw the birth announcements for the new baby. (4-10 yrs.)

• While Mother is in the hospital, have Dad bring notes home from the baby for the older child. These could include things like, "I cannot wait to come home and see you." (3-10 yrs.)

• A friend, Rebekah, enjoyed the "hello" message her new brother, Erik, sent home from the hospital. It was a tape recording of the new arrival crying. (3-10 yrs.)

• Take a photo of your older child with you to the hospital and tape it to the side of the baby's crib. When the older child comes to visit, he or she will be happy to see the new baby with the picture. (3-10 yrs.)

   • Have a birthday party for the baby when you come home from the hospital. The older child could have a present for the new arrival and the baby should definitely have something for the older child. This helps everyone get acquainted. (2-10 yrs.)

Give him a chance to hold his new sister.

at least it doesn't bark....

   • Some parents say that their school-age children resent the fact that the new baby gets to stay at home with mother while they attend school. They suggest putting a mailbox on the door to your child's room and filling it with notes about what you and the baby did during the day. Your child will feel less left out of your life when he or she opens the mail. (3-10 yrs.)

   • Do a special project with each child or take each one some-place special alone. It's good to do things together, but an occasional outing alone makes each child feel good about himself. (2-10 yrs.)

• Always recognize children's differences and help them to understand (and appreciate) each other. (2-10 yrs.)

Some Reading
Nobody Asked Me If I Wanted a Baby Sister, by Martha Alexander. (New York: Dial Press, 1971.) (3-6 yrs.)

Big Sister, Little Brother, by Terry Berger. (Milwaukee: Advanced Learning Concepts, 1974.) (4-10 yrs.)

Raising Cain (And Abel, Too): The Parents' Book of Sibling Rivalry, by John F. McDermott. (New York: Wyden Books, 1980.)

Anger
• A ranting child? Count to ten so he or she can cool off a little. The same goes for parents. (3-10 yrs.)

• Use up some of that angry energy. One father we know suggests having your child take out frustrations on a punching bag or a pillow. (3-10 yrs.)

• TANTRUMS! SCREAMS! TEARS! There's no soothing. Quick, grab a small cup and try to catch the tears. Your child will be giggling in a minute while eagerly trying to help you out. (2-8 yrs.)

• For screaming, try whispering. It's hard to hear someone who is whispering in your ear while you're yelling. My children always stop to listen to *our* secret. (2-10 yrs.)

• Some children handle anger by biting. Don't just stand there coaxing your child to let go. Elizabeth, a nursery school assistant, says: "Pinch the nose shut. The child will release the victim the moment the oxygen supply is cut off." Next: A lecture on biting.

• When Mom or Dad become involved in the argument, write out your anger and hand it to your child. Be sure that you include in the note that you will only pay attention to a written reply. Thinking up a reply will take some time—enough time hopefully for both parties to cool off. (8-10 yrs.)

Arguments
• After the sibling fight is over and bad feelings still exist, have your children "kiss and make-up." Once they start smiling and giggling and kiss, they are in a much better mood to discuss the argument. (3-10 yrs.)

• For an argument in progress, a big hug from a parent to one of the participants in the fighting match can be much more effective than trying to pull them apart and reason with them. Calm down, then discuss. (2-10 yrs.)

• Hugs are not only for breaking up fights. They are also for comforting someone who has had a bad day. I've found that it really breaks the ice and helps your child talk about what is bothering him or her. (3-10 yrs.)

• When the argument is only a verbal one, tell them that they have to sing their complaint, *and* their retorts. It's a fun way to end the argument. (3-10 yrs.)

• Some mothers sing commands to their children all the time. You'd be surprised how fast a child responds to a command when you sing it.

• A mother of an eight-year old warns, "Don't get involved in an argument about when it's time for a friend to leave. When the friend arrives, agree upon a time for him or her to go home, set the alarm clock, and you'll save a lot of bickering."

• When the standard, "but everyone else is" argument crops up, have your child make a list of reasons about why you should give in. (8-10 yrs.)

Respect for Self and Others
• Confidence and self-respect start young. They begin with the way parents love and care for the child—right from the cradle. Children understand through touching, holding, talking, and by listening to the tone of your voice.

• Words are powerful, remember that! Avoid judging, criticizing, or comparing. Each child is an individual.

• Don't make negative remarks about your children to your children, or when speaking about them with others.

• Sometimes, though, it's necessary to make a constructive criticism. Soften it by sandwiching between two compliments.

• A friend, Martha, has a calendar, and on that calendar she has a written reminder to say one thing she likes about her daughter, Emily, to her daughter, each day.

• Show an interest in what your children have to say. *Make* time to listen. Teach them how to listen to others, too. Explain the courtesy of not interrupting.

• Another way to develop a positive feeling about themselves is to keep photos of your children around the house.

• Display their artistic creations in prominent places in the house: on the mantel, bookshelf, or in a frame. Use them as center-pieces, too, especially when there's company for dinner.

• Encourage the development of skills your children show an ability for—not the skills *you* want them to have. Respect their interests and talents.

• Go out of your way to notice your child's presence. Silence can be misunderstood as rejection.

• Another way to en-courage positive feelings is to let your children choose their outfit for the day. The com-bination may look bad to you, but if your child thinks that he or she looks good, that's all that matters, for now. Clothing selections will improve as your child grows older. (See section on "Selection for In-dependence." (3-10 yrs.)

"I got dressed all by myself!"

• Children enjoy receiving mail. Seeing their names on an envelope or package is a self-respect builder. When ordering things for your children (books, free offers), use your child's name in the return address. No matter how young your children are, let them open their envelope or package. (3-10 yrs.)

• Consideration for privacy is also a form of respect. Put a door knocker on each child's bedroom door. This will be a reminder to knock before entering and will reinforce respect for privacy. (3-10 yrs.)

• Sharing is another resource for teaching respect for others. A mother we know offers this successful solution: Ask a visiting friend to bring along a few favorite toys. Both playmates will have something they *must* share, and the sharing won't be one-sided. (2-10 yrs.)

• For books to read along with your child, see the "Books to Read Along With Children" section, "Ourselves and Others."

For further understanding of your child's emotions

Feelings, by Creative Educational Society. (Mankato, 1971.) (3-5 yrs.)

How to Discipline with Love—from Crib to College, by Fitzhugh Dodson. (New York: Rawson, Wade Pubs., Inc., 1977.)

What Makes Me Feel This Way? Growing Up with Human Emotions, by Eda J. LeShan. (New York: MacMillan Publishing Co., Inc., 1972.) (6-10 yrs.)

Crow Boy, by Taro Yashima. (New York: Viking Press, Inc., 1955.) (multi-age picture book)

Your Child's Self-Esteem, the Key to His Life, by Dorothy Briggs. (New York: Doubleday & Co., Inc., 1970.)

76 *more* helpful hints on:

Soothing Solutions

Fears

• Talk about fear with your child. Explain the natural phenomena involved or teach your child to overcome the fear. For example, if he or she is afraid of water, teach your child to swim.

• If your child is frightened by loud noises, a barking dog or some other situation, you can help by acting calm and helping your child to get to know the thing he or she fears; but don't force a confrontation.

• Afraid of loud noises? Teach your child to cover his or her ears to muffle the sound.

• When night-time shadows take on frightening forms, take your child on a walk during the day and look at the shadows you make and those made by trees, etc. Experiment with daytime shadows, even have a shadow puppet show (see instructions for shadow puppets.) A little understanding will help lessen fears.

• Give your child a favorite stuffed animal and have your little one pretend he or she is reassuring the toy. Your child will end up by feeling better about the situation, too.

• There are monsters in my room! Your child's not exaggerating. To him or her, they're real. Tell your child that you are very strong, put up a really good fight, and throw those monsters out of the room forever. (You may not agree that one should acknowledge the presence of imaginary monsters. If so, tell your child monsters aren't real. They are only imaginary.)

• Every child knows the word *exit* from the program Sesame Street. Put an *exit* sign over the door and have all the monsters leave through the *exit*. (This really worked for a friend whose son was terrified by the pigs who had invaded his room.)

• Darkness is scary and being alone in the dark is extra frightening. Leave a night light on and the door open.

• Lessen your child's fear of thunder with the game "How many miles away was the thunder?" To play the game: When a flash appears in the sky, start counting *slowly*. When you hear the thunder, stop counting and you'll know how *very far away* the thunder was.

• Another thunder game is to have the child try to clap louder than the thunder.

Feeling Left Out

• Don't forget how important your attention is to a child; crabbiness is often a plea for some of that wonderful substance. A good way to provide some is to arrange a regular special time. The length and frequency can be determined by your schedule. Use the time to let your child be the boss. *You* do whatever *he or she* wants to do (within reason) for a set length of time. Let your child know that all of your attention belongs to him or her. (2-10 yrs.)

• Before a dinner party, have your children serve the hors d'oeuvres. Pack them a mini-meal with samples of what you are having for them to enjoy in their room. (3-10 yrs.)

• If your child is having a bad day and is very grumpy, telling your child how grouchy he or she is will not solve anything. Your child wants attention. Whenever your child is in one of these moods, tell him or her that you are going to dance the grumps away. Put on a record and dance all around. Your child will soon be jumping around and laughing—forgetting all about the mood and the boredom. (2-8 yrs.)

• Cabin Fever! You can't expect your child to play quietly all day long. Get out of the house. Go to the park or for a walk. If it's too cold, go to an enclosed shopping mall. There'll be lots of open space and it's a good place to use up that extra energy. For more ideas, see the "Places to Go" section. (2-10 yrs.)

• A very important point to remember is: Don't wait until your child whines and complains about being bored or feeling left out. Give attention as often as possible, especially when he or she is demonstrating behavior you approve of. Reinforce the acceptable behavior, don't react to and therefore encourage the undesirable. (NB-10 yrs.)

• When my daughter was almost a year old, she was in the habit of screaming and crying when awakening from a nap or from a night's sleep. To break the screaming habit, I would let her cry. I *never* went into her room while she screamed, but waited out of sight near the door. The moment there was that short pause between screams, I opened the door immediately and with a big smile said "hello." Those few seconds between screams may not sound like enough time to mold behavior, but she soon learned that screaming was not acceptable and On her own called out for Mommy or Daddy instead.

• See the "Books to Read Along With Children" section, "Special Feelings of Children."

Bedtime
• Things to Make the Night Less Dark

A cuddly toy	A night light
A canteen of water	A wind-up music box
A big hug	A glow-in-the-dark picture
Some songs you sang as a child	Soft music on a tape recorder

• Give your child a big hug and tuck him or her in *tightly* for a snug and secure feeling. (2-10 yrs.)

• Read a favorite story in bed. (1-10 yrs.)

• Poetry is especially good for bedtime reading since rhythm has a soothing and relaxing effect. Avoid all stories that are exciting because of their action. Fairy tales and all stories with a mystery element are examples. (2-10 yrs.)

• Something warm to drink helps to calm and quiet down before bed. (1-10 yrs.)

• Have the child put all his or her toys to bed, one by one. Then your child can be *last* and stay up the latest. (2-8 yrs.)

• Sing softly to your child. If he or she dozes off, wait—don't sneak out right away. It takes twenty minutes to fall asleep. (NB-10 yrs.)

• Tell about a special event for the next day and remind your sleepy little one that the faster he or she goes to sleep, the sooner tomorrow will come. (3-10 yrs.)

• Maintain a rule for the child: Once in bed, you stay in bed. Sometimes, if you feel that you put your child to bed too early, be flexible and allow for variations in sleeping patterns. Set a timer and read a book to him or her or do some other *quiet* activity. (Don't make this a habit.) (3-10 yrs.)

• See the "Books to Read Along With Children" section for a list of lullabies and sleepy stories to read to your young child.

Go To Bed; A Book of Bedtime Poems, compiled by L.B. Hopkins. (New York: Knopf, Alfred A., Inc., 1979.) (5-10 yrs.)

Moving

Chris, wife of a military doctor, is a veteran of many transfers. These are some of her successful moving secrets.

• Tell your child about the move as soon as you know. Let your child participate in selecting your new home and checking out the town. (3-10 yrs.)

• Write to the local Chamber of Commerce in your new town. They'll send you maps and information about important spots and facilities.

• Obtain a floor plan of the new house or draw one yourself. Let your child also have a drawing of his or her room to arrange furniture or draw in an arrangement with a pencil. When you do move, the house will not seem so unfamiliar. (3-10 yrs.)

• On a road map, show your child the location of the new house in relation to the old one. Let him or her keep the new map to carry along when you move. Your child can follow along as you drive or fly across states or countries. (4-10 yrs.)

• Have a good-bye party and let your child invite all his or her special friends. Exchange small gifts for remembrances and addresses and phone numbers to assure your child that he or she will not be completely cut off from friends. (3-10 yrs.)

• Load your child's things onto the moving van last so they will be unpacked first. (2-10 yrs.)

• When you get to a new city, find your pediatrician and dentist *before* you need them.

• Get in touch with the new school in your area and find out what records your child will need in addition to checking on what courses are offered.

• Ask your child to select a friend from the new school to come over for a visit.

To help your younger child understand

I'm Moving, by Martha Hickman. (Nashville, TN: Abingdon Press, 1974.) (3-6 yrs.)

Moving Day, by Tobi Tobias. (New York: Knopf, Alfred A., Inc., 1976.) (3-6 yrs.)

Aldo Applesauce, by Johanna Hurwitz. (New York: Morrow, William & Co., Inc., 1979.) (7-10 yrs.)

Big Hello, by Janet Schulman. (New York: Morrow, William & Co., Inc., 1976.) (5-8 yrs.)

Moving Molly, by Shirley Hughes. (Englewood Cliffs, N.J.: Prentice-Hall, Inc., 1978.) (3-6 yrs.)

When Mom and Dad Are Away

• Show your child on a map where you will be in relation to your home. (3-10 yrs.)

• When both parents are away from home, have the child keep a diary. The child will enjoy recording the day's events in pictures or by dictating to the sitter. In this way, the parents will be filled in on what happened while they were away. (3-10 yrs.)

• Steve, a father whose job requires a lot of travel, always sends postcards home to his children while he's away.

• If you have to be out of town, make a picture book showing where you are going.

• Number sheets of paper in a notebook for your child to tear off for each day you'll be away. (3-10 yrs.)

• Leave a goodie bag with one small gift or edible treat for the sitter to give to the child each day you are out of town. (2-10 yrs.)

• Leave an album with pictures of the family in it. This works especially well if you are going to be away for a few days. (2-10 yrs.)

• When friends of ours took a "parents only" vacation, they left a cassette recording of a bedtime story for each night they were away. Both parents took turns reading the story. They were sure to say "goodnight" and that they would be home very soon. (1-10 yrs.)

Special Hints for Busy Parents

• Involve your children in activities you enjoy, since your time with them and for yourself is limited. If you like to paint, let them paint their own pictures with you. If you like to sail, take them with you. Let them participate in activities you don't particularly enjoy, while you are at work. This makes your time together happier. (1-10 yrs.)

• In a home with working parents, have two calendars, one for notes to family, and the other for notations for yourself. Everyone will know where to check for messages and where to leave any information. (8-10 yrs.)

• Or have your child make a family mailbox. (8-10 yrs.)

• To decide on household priorities, all family members should make a list of everything to be done, then assign jobs. It's a good idea to rotate duties such as packing lunches, cleaning, laundry. (5-10 yrs.)

• Children are very interested in the places their parents work and in meeting the people you work with and talk about. Plan a visit to your office so your child will be familiar with the office and your colleagues. (2-10 yrs.)

• Plan to have a special time with your children at least two times a week, or more often if possible. Schedule it, so you will be sure to do it. Make sure that your child understands that occasionally his or her "appointment" must be re-scheduled. (5-10 yrs.)

• If your children are very young, schedule your housekeeping duties in the evenings when they are asleep, rather than doing all the work on the weekend when free-time should be spent with your family.

• Plan weekly menus and shop once a week, if possible.

• Cook elaborate meals on the weekend when you have more time. Prepare in larger quantities so you may freeze leftovers for a meal later in the week, or use leftovers from a large meal in a casserole or stew for a quick meal after work.

• Children can help plan menus, shop, and prepare meals. (8-10 yrs.)

• Lay out clothes, set the table, make lunches, and bathe in the evening. This will eliminate half of the morning rush. (3-10 yrs.)

• Have a specific location for books, lunches, brief cases, and other take-along necessities so you don't spend time searching for things in the morning.

For more information and help

Life with Working Parents; Practical Hints for Everyday Situations, by Esther Hautzig. (New York: Macmillan Publishing Co., Inc., 1976.(8-10 yrs.)

Help; A Handbook for Working Mothers, by Barbara Greenleaf. (New York: Crowell, Thomas Y., Co., 1978.)

Home Alone, by Eleanor Schick. (New York: Dial Press, 1980.) (4-8 yrs.)

My Mom Got a Job, by Lucia Smith. (New York: Holt, Rinehart & Winston, Inc., 1979.) (4-7 yrs.)

Homework

• Set aside a specific time and place for homework. It's a perfect exercise for teaching children not only schoolwork but how to organize their own time and activities. (7-10 yrs.)

• Make special long-term homework projects the topic of family dinners. This helps the child feel his project is important and discussion makes him or her think out what has to be done and how to do it. Other members of the family enjoy it too. (7-10 yrs.)

• Keep the homework area away from the television. (7-10 yrs.)

• Save some paperwork from the office or from the household, and work along with your child as he or she works. One father we know always balances the checkbook and pays the bills during homework time. The child realizes that everyone has duties that he or she must perform, and if a homework question arises, there's always advice nearby. (7-10 yrs.)

• Parents should be available for help, but only upon request, and then sparingly. (7-10 yrs.)

• Encourage your child to have a homework notebook, or use a small pocket calendar in which he or she can write down assignments and the date due. (7-10 yrs.)

• When your child has no homework assignments, have him or her spend the scheduled study time reading a book. (7-10 yrs.)

• Some children work better with people around rather than isolated in a room where they can doodle and daydream. See if being with the family crowd makes a difference. (7-10 yrs.)

T.V. Watching

• Have puzzles, manipulative toys, building toys, electronic games, and art materials near the T.V. Children will begin playing and spend less time "glued" to T.V. (2-10 yrs.)

• Don't tell children they can't watch television. Simply involve them in a new activity that takes them away from it. This makes television less enticing. (2-10 yrs.)

• Have regular hours for watching television. When they do watch, try to watch with them and discuss the program. When you can't watch with them, ask them to relate the story of the program to you. This will help them organize sequences of events in their own mind and make the television an educational tool. (4-10 yrs.)

• Most parents of older children agreed that night-time T.V. is a big problem. One solution was to watch T.V. on weekends only unless there was something very special on during the week. (7-10 yrs.)

• Another parent suggested reading the T.V. guide together, and that the whole family plan their T.V. viewing for the week. (7-10 yrs.)

• Your older child doesn't like to be lectured to about T.V. Make comments about the program to your spouse or other family member that can inadvertently be overheard. (8-10 yrs.)

• When something is presented on T.V. that is in opposition to the family's values or offends it in any way, many parents advocate loud verbal reactions and exclamations of disapproval. (2-10 yrs.)

• Adapt your movie-going techniques to your television viewing:
1. Decide what to see.
2. Find out about the content.
3. Leave the theater (shut off the T.V.) if not appropriate.
4. Discuss the movie (T.V. program) afterwards.

• Some lessons learned from movie-going families:
1. Select programs as you would plan a week's menu.
2. Critically evaluate T.V. content—encourage your children to discuss it, too.
3. Let T.V. programs lead to discussions on other topics. (4-10 yrs.)

• To help you select appropriate programs for your children, you can get on the mailing list for NBC's "Viewer's Guides," part of their Project Peacock. These guides, mailed to you periodically, give you an introduction to upcoming children's series on NBC and suggest practical ways for you to use them with your family. Each Project Peacock Viewer's Guide will give you a plot synopsis and questions about the story. To get on the mailing list write to:

Dr. Ellen Rodman
Director, Children's Informational
 Services
National Broadcasting Corporation
30 Rockefeller Plaza
New York, New York 10112
(212) 664-5443

• The National PTA has been very concerned about violence in television programming. Write to the national office for their annual "TV Program Review Guide," or call their TV Action Center for further information on how you can help improve children's programs and make television-watching more educational in your own home. The TV Action Center's toll free telephone number is 800-621-4114 (Illinois residents use 800-572-7891). To receive the "TV Program Review Guide" write to:

The National PTA
700 North Rush St.
Chicago, IL 60611
(312) 787-0977

Helpful Books and Publications:

How to Treat T.V. with TLC, by ACT Guide to Children's Televison. (Boston: Beacon Press, Inc., 1977)

Family Guide to Children's Television, by Evelyn Kay. (New York: Pantheon Books, 1974.)

Watching Television with Your Children, by Eda J. Leshan, available from American Broadcasting Companies, Inc., 1330 Avenue of the Americas, New York, New York 10019

49 *more* helpful hints on:

Everyday Learning

Games Make It Fun

• Make a map of a room in your house. Put all the furniture and doorways on it. Have your child close his or her eyes while you hide an object in the room. Return to your child and point on the map where you have hidden the object. Let him or her follow the map and find it. Reverse the game and let your child hide the object. (4-8 yrs.)

• Mix playdough colors together and guess what colors they will make. (Playdough recipe in the Craft Recipe section.) Have all the primary colors available. When you're done, help make new colors into different objects. One good suggestion is to have your child make playdough food for his or her kitchen. (2-4 yrs.)

• Let your children sort the laundry with you. This will help them learn the names of colors as you sort out lights and darks. (2-3 yrs.)

• Matching pairs is a good learning exercise. Gather up a number of household items of which you have at least two and let the child match them. You can also play matching games with shapes, colors, sizes, and functions. (2-6 yrs.)

• Look around a room and see how many different shapes you can find. A bookshelf has rectangles and squares, a sofa pillow is a circle, etc.

• Put a familiar object into a box or a bag. Have your child reach in and guess what the object is without removing it from the box. After he or she guesses, put another object in and start the game again.

• Try this game with several objects in the bag or box. Vary the size and number according to the age of the child. (3-10 yrs.)

• Give your child an empty egg carton and a tray containing several similar and different small objects such as peas, beans, buttons, keys, etc. Let your child put like objects into the same section of the egg carton. (3-5 yrs.)

• Take three or four of your child's baby puzzles and mix all the pieces together. It will be quite a challenge to make three puzzles at once. (3-7 yrs.)

For more imaginative games and activities

Living and Learning with Children, by Paula Jorde (Washington: Acropolis Books, Ltd., 1981.)

Great Perpetual Learning Machine; Being a Stupendous Collection of Ideas, Games, Experiments, Activities, and Recommendations for Further Exploration, by Jim Blake. (New York: Little, Brown & Co., 1976.) (5-10 yrs.)

See the "Books to Read Along With Children" section, "Pictures to Talk About" for a list of books to read along with your child. (3-5 yrs.)

Letters and Numbers

• A simple game of labeling is a wonderful way to enrich your baby's vocabulary. Make it a habit to name things for your child as you encounter them. (NB-2 yrs.)

Give him labels for objects in the house-after he reads them, he can attach them.

(If you can stand it, leave the labels on for awhile to reinforce the learning.)

• Place familiar pictures under the plastic covers of a photo album. It's easy for your child to turn the pages. You can make a new book when he or she tires of this one. A great vocabulary builder too! (1-3yrs.)

• Your older child can create his or her own book. Staple several sheets of paper together to make a picture book. When your child's done, have him or her dictate the story for you to record. An older child can record his or her own story. (3-10 yrs.)

• Make your own family newspaper/newsletter. Let your children write or dictate the news stories, fill it with original illustrations, make photocopies and mail out the news to all their friends or even to Grandma and Grandpa instead of a letter. (3-10 yrs.)

• "Read" a store catalogue with your child. This is an excellent way to improve your child's vocabulary since so many different things are pictured there. (2-5 yrs.)

• "Guess what I'm doing"—a simple charades games, can also use a child's favorite book titles, animals, etc. (3-10 yrs.)

• Opposites: Take turns calling out words to which the other person responds as quickly as possible with the word's opposite. A similar game can be played with rhyming words. (4-10 yrs.)

• Play "Guess what I'm thinking of . . . It's brown." After each guess, add another clue. Don't make the object too difficult to guess until the child is older. (3-10 yrs.)

• Put your old typewriter (or one you buy at a garage sale) out permanently for children to type on. Those who haven't learned to read and write will create words, while those who can, will pour out their imaginings freely and happily. It's a good communication device. (3-10 yrs.)

• Alphabet noodles are good letter practice. Your child can glue the letters of the alphabet in order on a sheet of paper. With a more advanced child, make simple words. He or she can also practice numbers in the same way with the numbers that come mixed in with the letters. (3-6 yrs.)

• Cut out shapes that make letters such as half circles and long and short lines. Let your child experiment making the letters of the alphabet. (3-6 yrs.)

• For practice in writing the letters of the alphabet, dictate your grocery list to your child, or have him or her write out any reminders such as "Call to make a dental appointment." Spell out any words your child does not know. (7-10 yrs.)

• Keep a journal. Young children can draw in it daily, while the older child can record not only the days' happenings, but also ideas and feelings. (3-10 yrs.)

• Plan that for a certain length of time, anything that anyone wants to say must be written out. It's fun and good practice. (7-10 yrs.)

• Have spelling bees. (7-10 yrs.)

• To help with math, cut out numbers from one to ten and place them in a bag or box. Let the child select any two numbers and add them and then subtract them. (4-10 yrs.)

• Play dominoes for more number practice. (4-10 yrs.)

• For more practice, see the section on "Books to Read Along With Children," "Learning Concepts," for a listing of books to read to your child.

• As a reference for parents, see the "Sources for Parent and Child" section, "About Play and Learning."

Science and Nature

• Have your child start a collection. He or she may collect rocks, fingerprints, insects, coins, shells, buttons, stamps, bottle caps, corks, keys, or postcards, Keep the collection in a personal museum. (3-10 yrs.)

• Several magnets and a box filled with familiar objects can provide a lot of fun. Some of the objects should be things a magnet will attract. Others can be cotton balls, wood, or a plastic spoon. Experiment and see which items adhere to the magnet. After you have discussed your findings, walk around the house and see if your child can guess if the magnet will stick to objects you find on the way. This is a fun game to play with friends, too. (4-8 yrs.)

• Fill your sink with water and let your child discover which objects will float and which will sink. Use everyday household things: corks, rocks, plastic lids, and crayons. (2-5 yrs.)

• Look for fingerprints with a magnifying glass. When your children discover them, try transfering some. If the print is on a dark surface, have them sprinkle a little talcum powder on the print and brush away the excess with a feather. On a light surface, sprinkle lead-pencil shavings over the print (use sandpaper to get shavings). To lift the print, place cellophane tape over the dusted surface. Lift the tape and stick it to a piece of paper. Have your children look at all the different shapes thumbprints come in, and let them figure out whose fingerprints they are. (4-10 yrs.)

• After you make the Jack-O-Lantern on Halloween, plant the pumpkin seeds and see them grow. Beans are easy to grow, too. Sprout them first in a jar with a damp cloth. Your child will be interested in seeing how the seeds split and send out sprouts. For instructions on sprouting seeds, see the "Fun Foods, Naturally" section. (4-10 yrs.)

• Egg cups, muffin tins, and quart milk cartons with the top half cut off make good containers for your child to plant seeds in and to watch them grow.

• There are always a few unpopped kernels when you make popcorn. Plant them in the top of an egg carton with a little soil. (4-10 yrs.)

• Each Spring, my son and I make a visit to a nursery. He selects a plant or two to be his summer pets. He has learned a lot about plant care, and always introduces his pets to friends. (3-7 yrs.)

• An older child will enjoy having his or her garden. Reserve a section of your garden, or a sunny spot in the yard. It will be a lot of fun planting, watering, and caring for the garden. Plant flowers, too, not just vegetables. (7-10 yrs.)

• See the "Books to Read Along With Children" section, "The Natural World," for a listing of books to read along with your young child.

Science Book, by Sara Bonnett Stein. (New York: Workman Publishing Co., Inc, 1979.) (5-10 yrs.)

Books for Young Explorers, issued by the National Geographic Society such as *Honeybees,* by J. Lecht, or *Blue Whale* by D.K. Grosvenor.

Music

• Save bottle caps. When you have five or six, punch a hole in the center with a nail and string them on some cord. Shake and listen to their music. (2-10 yrs.)

• Listen to classical music with your child. Play an imagination game. Ask him or her, "What do you think is happening in this music?" You'll be surprised at what your child comes up with. (3-10 yrs.)

• Find a class, or ask a local music instructor if he or she would be interested in forming a group music theory class. Both my son and Loel's daughter have absorbed a lot in their child-oriented group class, and an interest in music has been sparked. (4-8 yrs.)

• Form a kitchen band—if your ears can stand it. Two pan lids for cymbals; a wooden spoon and a pan for a drum; and an empty coffee can for bongos. (2-7 yrs.)

• Cover a comb with waxed paper and let your child blow through the paper to make music. (3-10 yrs.)

• Fill a small can with beans or buttons. Tape it *tightly* shut, and your child has maracas. (2-10 yrs.)

• To make a guitar, cut a hole in the lid of a shoe box. Wrap several rubber bands around the box and lid and over the hole. Let your child strum away. (2-10 yrs.)

• Another fun and inexpensive instrument your child can make is a kazoo. Attach waxed paper to one end of an empty toilet paper or paper towel roll with a rubber band. Have your child hum a tune into this new instrument. (2-10 yrs.)

• At age nine or ten, your child will be ready and interested in music lessons.

• See "Books to Read Along With Your Children" section, "Songs and Games."

Additional suggestions on music for your children:

Creative Movement for the Developing Child; A Nursery School Handbook for Non-Musicians, by Clare Cherry. (Belmont, CA: Pitman Learning Inc., 1971.) (3-5 yrs.)

What Shall We Do and Allee Galloo, Play Songs and Singing Songs for Young Children, by Marie Winn. (New York: Harper & Row Pubs., Inc., 1970.) (3-6 yrs.)

Making Musical Things: Improvised Instruments, by Ann Wiseman. (New York: Scribners, Charles, Sons, 1979.) (4-10 yrs.)

114 *more* helpful hints on:

Arts, Crafts and Activities

Activities Guide
Infants
Play materials that appeal to the senses and muscles:

soft playthings for throwing
light plastic blocks
washable, unbreakable doll
tinkling bells, musical rattle
tissue paper for rattling or tearing
squeaky play animals without removable mechanism

nests of hollow blocks or boxes to pull apart and put together
empty containers with removable lids to take off and put on
playthings in boxes or baskets for putting-in and taking-out
floating bath animals

Toddlers

Play materials that challenge growing powers:

large, soft ball to push, lie on, or roll over

large colored nesting blocks (with rope handles in the side) to serve for piling up, for seats to sit on, for boxes to put things in, for conveyors for dragging

cartons or wooden boxes (without nails or splinters) to climb upon or into; hollow barrel to crawl through

plank, slightly raised at one or both ends, to walk on, bounce on, and jump off

large hollow blocks and small floor blocks to carry and pile up

sand pile with bucket, scoop, and other sand playthings

wagon or truck to ride in

small rocking horse or rolling horse

play materials for reliving what has been enjoyed in real life, such as household articles, unbreakable dishes, simple, sturdy garden tools, autos, planes, doll, stroller, telephone, small chair

well-made picture books with many pictures, simple stories, nursery rhymes, scrapbooks

large crayons for marking

cuddly play animals

tom-tom, bells, music box

Two-year old

Play materials for developing large muscles:

barrel to climb through and roll over

Kiddie Kar

large hollow blocks to carry and pile up

steps for climbing

large balls

push-and-pull play materials

Play materials for pretending:

housekeeping equipment

washable, unbreakable doll

cuddly play animals

costume box with such simple properties as hat, purse, tie

ride-a-stick horse

Threes-Fours-Fives

Play materials, games, and apparatus for strengthening large muscles:

climbing tower, turning bars

crawling-through apparatus

wagon (large enough to hold a child)

tricycle (of correct size)

bouncing horse

push-and-pull play materials for younger children

jump ropes for older children

large balls

paddle with ball attached

beanbags

simple throwing games

simple rolling games

ten pins

large hollow blocks

mallet with peg set for younger children, work bench with real tools for older children

large floor blocks to lug and carry and to build large structures

Play materials that stretch the mind:

viewmaster with slides, filmstrips

globes for older children

books with simple stories, poems, jingles, nursery rhymes

picture books

lock with key

magnet

aquarium, terrarium

water play materials

bubble set

inlay puzzles, 8-20 pieces

matching games

Play materials for representative play:

washable, unbreakable doll that can be dressed and undressed

housekeeping equipment of all sorts including cooking, laundering, gardening

costume box for "dress-up" clothes

space hat

assorted floor blocks with small family figures

play luggage

farm and zoo animal sets

transportation play materials; boats, trucks, planes, trains, autos

steering wheel

ride-a-stick horse

sheet or blanket for play tent

large cartons for making stores, houses, stations and for climbing into

assorted blocks with animal and family figures, trucks, and other transportation vehicles

Play materials for expressing feelings:

crayons

painting materials with large brush and paper

hand-painting materials

blunt scissors and paste

clay

hammer, nails and soft wood

large wooden beads for younger children, smaller beads for older ones

sand and sand-play materials

wading or swimming pool

rocking chair

cuddly play animals

puppets (stick and hand)

musical top, music box, record player

percussion instruments such as: tom-tom, bells, triangle, finger cymbals

space hat, fireman's hat, workman's helmet

Sixes-Sevens-Eights

Play materials, games, and apparatus for strengthening the muscles and developing skills:

trapeze, horizontal ladder

climbing apparatus (knotted rope, rope ladder, climbing tower)

tumbling mat

tire swing

punching bag

balls, beanbag games, ring toss games

jump ropes, hoops, marbles, pogo stick, kite

bicycle, wagon, sled, skates

swimming accessories such as life jackets, inflatable animals for water play

garden tools and speed jackets

Play materials and games for stretching the mind:

magnets, thermometer, magnifying glass, soap bubble set, balloons

clock dial, abacus, cash register, weighing scales, number games

anagrams, lotto, alphabet sets, printing sets, typewriter, puzzles including map inlay puzzles

checkers, parcheesi

viewmaster, slides, films, filmstrips

globe of the world

chalkboard, flannel board

books: some to read, some for being read to (poetry and stories)

Play materials for make-believe:

playhouse easily converted into store, school, theater, club room

costumes for "dressing-up"

dollhouse, doll furniture

boy and girl dolls

dolls from other parts of the world

transportation vehicles: boats, trains, planes, dump trucks, tractors

play circus

puppets

Play materials to satisfy that urge to create and to express feelings:

crayons, paint, colored chalk to use on paper

materials for paper sculpture, clay

sewing kit including cloth for making doll clothes, tape measure

simple weaving materials

workbench with real tools

construction sets, design blocks

melody bells, resonator bells

marimba, xylophone

percussion instruments

record player

Nines-Tens-Elevens

Materials for developing teamwork and for contributing to "club" interests:

baseball, bat, gloves

basketball equipment

football

tennis ball and racquet

badminton set

table tennis set

croquet set

shuffleboard

gardening tools

camping equipment

beach and water balls

Games and apparatus for maintaining muscle tone and for perfecting skills:

trapeze, horizontal ladder, rings

climbing rope

tether ball, boxing gloves

dodgeball

bicycle, skates (roller and ice)

skis, sled

jump rope

Materials for creating and for building confidence and self esteem:

clay, paints, crayons

craft sets: leather, plastic, metal, stenciling on fabric

shell jewelry set

basket making

beadwork

tools, lumber, and wheels for making vehicles boys or girls can drive

models for making rockets, planes, trucks, ships

fishing equipment

camera

puppets

character dolls and materials for making doll clothes

harmonica

musical instruments (at this age children are interested in music lessons)

record player

Materials for stretching the mind:

microscope, magnifying glass, binoculars, telescope

batteries, electrical bell, switches, electrical cord

strong magnets

kite

meter stick, tape measure (steel and cloth), number line, protractor

stopwatch, electric clock, alarm clock, sundial, 3-minute egg glass

speedometer, micrometer, barometer

scales

compass

models of geometric figures

chess, dominoes, checkers

slides, films, filmstrips, globe, maps, chalkboard
hobby sets: stamp collector's album, rock-hound sets
jigsaw puzzles

books of reference: simple science and math, travel, exploration, adventure, discovery, invention
typewriter
live pets

Reprinted by permission by The Association of Childhood Education International from "PLAY: Children's Business."

Association for Childhood Education, International
3615 Wisconsin Avenue, N.W.
Washington, D.C. 20016
(202) 363-6963

Things to Save

Fabric scraps
String
Yarn
Buttons
Spools
Feathers
Ribbons
Wrapping paper
"Stamps" (from magazine ads)
Empty boxes
Cans
Fruit juice cans
Magazines
Cardboard tubes
Beads

Styrofoam meat trays
Egg cartons
Wallpaper sample books
Plastic gallon milk containers
Pint berry boxes
Aluminum pie tins
Feathers
Corks
Shoe polish applicators
Net bags from citrus fruit
Bottle caps
Old greeting cards
Sea shells
Wrapping paper
Popsicle sticks

Things to Have on Hand

Crayons
Pencils
Paints and brushes
Paste
Paper doilies
Scissors
Pipe cleaners
Popsicle sticks
Stapler
Tape
Cotton swabs
Cotton balls
Construction paper
Dried beans, rice, noodles

Chalk
Felt tip pens
Sponges
Cookie cutters
Glue
Clothespins (spring-type or straight)
Glitter
Sequins
Food coloring
Paper hole punch
Rollers (hair)
Toothpicks
Paper towels

Tips
Hints from our nursery school teachers:

• Cut the sleeves from an old raincoat. Put it on backwards and your child has a new painting smock that offers a lot of protection.

• Mix liquid soap with your tempera paints to make the colors wash out easier.

• If you decide to purchase magic markers for your child, buy those that are water-soluble.

• Store felt-tipped pens in a sealed jar so they won't dry out.

• Ashtrays are good to use for water dishes when painting. Use a double suction disc to avoid spills. There's even a place to rest your brush.

• Cut a hole in the center of a sponge and place the paint jar inside. The jar won't tip over, and the sponge will catch the drips.

• Another no-spill method is to cut holes in an inverted shallow box and place the paint jars inside the holes.

• Don't let your playdough dry out. Wrap it in foil and store it in an air-tight container.

• To keep modeling clay soft, close it in an air-tight container with a piece of damp cloth. This is also the method to soften hard clay.

• Remove the print from egg cartons you want to use for craft projects by wiping them with a piece of cotton soaked in rubbing alcohol.

• For a child who has trouble squeezing glue or paste from its container, put some glue in one of the sections of an empty egg carton and use cotton swabs or a paint brush to apply the glue. Fill the other sections of the egg carton with beans, cheerios, or rice. Your child can make a picture by gluing these foods to a stiff piece of paper or cardboard. (3-8 yrs.)

• Use the pages from a discontinued wallpaper sample book in several ways: wallpaper a doll's house; paint on it; fingerpaint on the back of the pages; or use it to create a scrapbook. (2-10 yrs.)

• Use an old cookie sheet for a magnetic board.

• Assemble a puzzle on a desk blotter. When it's time to set the dinner table, your child can cart the project away without breaking it apart. (4-10 yrs.)

• For practice with needle and thread, place the fabric in an embroidery hoop. It's easier to handle than a floppy piece of cloth. (5-10 yrs.)

• A wonderful source of paper is a print shop. They have scraps in many sizes and colors, ocasionally free but always cheap, and sometimes made into small, interesting, odd-shaped pads. (2-10 yrs.)

• In addition to the refrigerator door, display artwork on the inside of the basement door, or on the outside of kitchen cabinets.

Keep It Neat

• L o e l's daughter, Jessica, enjoys doing artwork on all sizes of paper. Her mother made it convenient for both of them by placing a roll of butcher paper on a mounted dowel rod. She can cut off as much paper as needed or paint on it as it hangs down. (3-10 yrs.)

• Our nursery school uses shoe polish applicators in addition to paint brushes for artwork.

• Cover a piece of masonite with clear plastic adhesive paper and

Butcher paper mounted on wall

old vinyl tablecloth

use it for finger painting. While the paint is still wet, press a sheet of clean paper over the top of it and you have a mono-print—and you've saved a lot of money by not buying expensive finger-painting paper. (2-8 yrs.)

• Mix paints in empty juice cans. (12 oz.) Powdered paints work best. You can also mix paints in empty baby food jars. When your child is finished, the jars can be sealed. Be careful though, because glass jars are easily broken.

• Put spoonfuls of different colored paints on styrofoam meat trays. The paints won't penetrate, and your child will have an artist's palette. Cut a hole in one corner of the tray to slip a thumb through! (4-10 yrs.)

• Keep the easel well stocked with paper and paints or magic markers and crayons, and in a place where paint won't damage anything. An always-prepared easel gives children an instant creative outlet. (3-10 yrs.)

• Chocolate pudding makes good and delicious finger paint.

• Ketchup works too, but it's not as tasty.

• Invert a tin can, punch a hole in it with a can opener, then place your child's scissors in the hole, for safe storage.

• My children use a plastic silverware tray to hold their art supplies. One section can be for pens, another for crayons, yet another for scissors and tape.

Things To Make

• Tape two empty toilet paper rolls together lengthwise to make "binoculars." Add a string so that your child can hang them around his or her neck. (2-6 yrs.)

• Cut away the handle-side and the top spout portion of a plastic gallon jug of milk. Have your child decorate it with buttons, pipe cleaners, or anything else you may have, for a space helmet. (3-10 yrs.)

• Make a boat out of an old styrofoam meat tray with a straw for a mast and a napkin for a sail. Use it in the bathtub or pool. (3-6 yrs.)

• Half a walnut shell makes a boat, too. Put a toothpick in for a mast and make a paper sail. (4-7 yrs.)

• Fill a clear plastic bag with different things you have around the house, such as cotton balls, paper clips, noodles, or ribbon. Inflate the filled bag, tie it shut, attach it to a stick, and your child has created a personal air collage. (3-6 yrs.)

• To make a butterfly, push a napkin or half a paper towel in the opening of a clothespin—not the squeeze type—to form the wings. Add a pipe cleaner for antennae and paint the eyes. (3-6 yrs.)

• Take your children on a rock-hunting walk. When you get home, ask what animal each rock looks like. Have your children paint them and make their own rock animals. (3-10 yrs.)

A decorated baby-wipe carton can become a penny bank ←

• Cut the bottom of an empty egg carton in half lengthwise, turn it over, and you have two caterpillars. Color them and help your child add pipe cleaner antennae. (3-6 yrs.)

• Save cardboard boxes to make a city. Draw a town map on a large sheet of poster board. The kids can decorate it with flowers, grass, sidewalks, and streets; set up box buildings, and drive toy cars around. (2-10 yrs.)

• Instead of posterboard, our friends, Kelley and Kerry, build their city on a fold-up cutting board made for sewing. After play, it folds up for easy storage. (2-10 yrs.)

• Plastic hand lotion or laundry soap containers make wonderful puppet heads. Help your child make a simple dress with arms for the body. Decorate the "head" with hair and make a "face" by drawing one on white paper and pasting it on the front. (3-10 yrs.)

• Cut the fingers off an old pair of gloves and the fingertips become tiny puppets. Add button eyes, yarn hair, or anything else to make the finger puppets come alive. (4-10 yrs.)

• Paint a face on a clothespin (not the squeeze type); add or paint on clothing and you have a puppet. (4-10 yrs.)

• Cut two holes in an inverted grocery bag. Let these be the eyes. Then let your child complete the face. Yarn can be used for the hair. When it is complete, let your child slip the bag over his or her head and wear it as a mask. Use your collective imagination; the mask can be an animal, too. (2-6 yrs.)

• Printmaking is easy when you carve a picture on the bottom of a styrofoam meat tray with a dried-out pen. Spread paint on the bottom and print. (4-10 yrs.)

• Carrots or potatoes can be used to make prints. Carve a design in them with a knife. (Mom or Dad should help out with this one.) (3-10 yrs.)

• Squeeze glue over a sheet of paper. Before it dries, sprinkle dyed sand or cookie sprinkles; add scraps of fabric or cotton balls, and your child has a unique collage. (3-8 yrs.)

• Save wooden spools from thread—they can be painted, strung on elastic cord to make jewelry, made into dollhouse furniture, or glued together to make sculptures. (18 mo.-10 yrs.)

• Your older child can use spools to fashion chess pieces. (8-10 yrs.)

• Plan a craft project that can't be completed in one day. An empty doll house will soon be filled by all sorts of creative furniture and decorations. Let the children decorate their own dollhouse instead of buying lots of expensive accessories. (8-10 yrs.)

• Or have your children assemble model kits. (8-10 yrs.)

• Butterick makes patterns for children to make. Each pattern in the series teaches sewing basics and is increasingly difficult. A great way to teach children to sew. (8-10 yrs.)

• Your child can create "modern art" by dipping pieces of string in different colors of paint and streaking them across a sheet of paper. (4-10 yrs.)

Craft books for your young child
Little Kids' Craft Book, by Jackie Vermeer. (New York: Taplinger Publishing Co., Inc., 1973.) (2-5 yrs.)

Look At This, by Harlow Rockwell. (New York: Macmillan Publishing Co., Inc., 1978.) (7-10 yrs) and *I Did It,* by Harlow Rockwell. (New York: Macmillan, 1974.) (7-10 yrs.)

For your older child
Making Things: The Handbook of Creative Discovery, by Ann Wiseman. (Boston: Little Brown & Co., 1973.) (5-10 yrs.)

Craft Recipes
• *Play Dough:* 3 cups flour, 1 1/2 cups salt, 6 teaspoons cream of tartar, 3 cups water and food coloring, 3 T cooking oil. Mix dry ingre-

dients together. Mix wet ingredients together. Blend both batches, then stir over low heat until it forms a ball. Knead a bit and let cool. Store in plastic container. It lasts and lasts and lasts. (2-7 yrs.)

• *Edible Play Dough:* 1 cup peanut butter, 1/2 cup milk powder, 1/2 cup wheat germ, 1/4 cup honey. Stir together. If sticky, add more milk powder. Use as regular play dough to create faces, pots, balls, and dolls. Decorate with raisins, coconut, vegetable sticks, bean sprouts, or red hot candies. (18 mos.-7 yrs.)

• *Inedible Bakers Clay Dough:* 4 cups unsifted flour, 1 cup salt, 1 1/2 cups water. Combine all ingredients in a bowl, mixing with a wooden spoon. Knead for 4-6 minutes. Use corn kernels, lentils, black-eyed peas, alphabet soup, cloves, peppercorns, licorice, or rice to decorate "cookies." Preheat oven to 350°F. Bake for one hour but check occasionally because they may take less time. When cool, brush with a yellow egg glaze. Shellac them if you wish to keep them for several years. (4-10 yrs.)

• *Oven Art:* This is the same recipe as Inedible Clay Dough, but instead of decorating the dough, use cookie cutters or shape it into imaginary objects. Bake at 350°F. for about 15 minutes. Depending on the size of your child's creation, it may take a few minutes more or less. Paint the new "toys" after they've cooled, and shellac to preserve. (4-10 yrs.)

• *Paste:* 1 cup flour plus 1/2 cup water.

• *More durable paste:* 1/2 cup flour added to 1 cup boiling water.

• *Finger Paint:* Mix an equal amount of liquid detergent or laundry starch with food coloring or paint. (2-8 yrs.)

• *Bubble Soap:* Mix 1/3 cup liquid detergent to 2/3 cup water. Bend a piece of wire to make a blower.

• *Depression Garden:* Glass or plastic bowl (preferably clear) about 7" in diameter and 3" deep. Broken pieces of coal, porous brick, clay flower pot or sponge, bluing, salt, ammonia, vegetable coloring and water.
Soak pieces of coal, flower pot, brick, sponge or other porous material in water until saturated. Place the porous material in the bowl to form the base for the formation. Over this material, sprinkle 2 T water, 2 T sale, 2 T bluing. The next day, add 2 more T salt. On the third day, pour into the bottom of the bowl—not directly on the base material, 2 T each of salt, water, and bluing; add 2 T household ammonia. At this time, add a few drops of food coloring or colored ink

directly to the base material to give it color, if you wish. To keep the formation "growing," add more bluing, water and salt from time to time. Do not pour anything directly on the formation. A free circulation of air is necessary. Formations will develop more rapidly when the air is dry. Keep this out of reach of little brothers and sisters. **IT'S POISON!** (4-10 yrs.)

• *Papier Maché:* Tear newspaper into small pieces. Place the shredded paper into a rust-free container, cover with hot water, and soak overnight. Tear it up more and squeeze out the excess water. Add starch, flour, or wallpaper paste to the mixture until it is firm enough to model. Keep in a cool place for a few days. Use it like clay. Let the artwork dry and sponge with clear shellac. (6-10 yrs.)

• *Modeling Dough:* 1 cup salt, 1/2 cup cornstarch, 2/3 cup water. Cook over a low flame, stirring constantly until the mixture thickens. Remove from heat, cool, and knead in food coloring. Make beads, Christmas tree ornaments and doll and doll house foods and accessories. (4-10 yrs.)

• *Glop:* This is gooey, drippy, slimy, repulsive, fascinating material that stretches see-through thin, pats pudgy thick, and can be cut with scissors. Start with about 1/4 (one fourth) cup white glue (a little goes a long way), and slowly add liquid starch until it congeals and pulls away easily from the container. The amount of starch necessary for coagulation seems to vary with the weather, but you will probably need at least 1/4 (one fourth) cup of starch. If you like, add a few drops of food coloring for a splashy effect.
    NOTE: The glue dough is toxic—not to be used with children who cannot keep it out of their mouths—and will not last much more than a day. (3-10 yrs.)

• *Emergency Paint:* If rainy days catch you with a watercolor set bogged in murky browns, try this last gasp mix: 3 heaping tablespoons powdered milk, 1 tablespoon flour, 8 to 10 drops of food coloring and 5 to 6 tablespoons of water. The powdered milk gives the paint a glistening effect, particularly pretty on construction paper.
    If you're out of powdered milk, you can make the paint anyway: Increase the flour to 3 tablespoons and decrease the food coloring to 5 to 6 drops. This is not the stuff that made Rembrandt great, but it will get you through the afternoon. (3-10 yrs.)

• *Cornstarch Dough:* This is a fine sculpting dough, drying to a hard surface. It also vacuums up easily if the pieces pulverize. Mix 1 cup cornstarch and 2 cups baking soda together in a saucepan until blended. Add 1 1/4 cups cold water and, if you like, a few drops of food coloring. Stir until smooth. Cook over medium heat until boiling, stirring constantly. Boil a minute or so until the mixture looks like mashed potatoes and pulls away easily from the pan. Turn out on the counter and cool for several minutes; then knead until smooth. This dough may be used to make beautiful jewelry:

Beads: Roll dough into balls, varying the size. Pierce each ball with a toothpick, working it around to make a good hole. Let bead dry in a warm oven for five to six hours or overnight. Gently remove the toothpick and paint the bead if you want. String with a tapestry or crewel needle and a double strand of extra-strong button or carpet thread.

Bracelet/Armband: A child who can roll out a thin "snake" can make this. Pinch the ends of the "snake" together, or overlap. Let dry five to six hours in a warm oven, or overnight. Paint.

Pin: Make a ball and mash it into a circle. Decorate with other bits of dough, pressing them gently to make sure they adhere to the surface. Attach a safety pin to the back of the circle with a dab of dough. Let dry, then paint.

Flower Stand: If the child is too young to manage a "snake," try making an interesting lump and coating it with an egg wash (one beaten egg with one tablespoon water). Poke a few holes in the lump with a toothpick and let it dry overnight in a warm oven. When the lump is dry, stick a few straw flowers in the holes. This makes an attractive gift, providing a happy outlet for the child's natural generosity. (3-10 yrs.)

For more recipes
Recipes for Art and Craft Materials, by Helen Sattler. (New York: Lothrop, Lee & Shephard Books, 1973.)

Things To Do
• Set up a grocery store with such items as empty cereal boxes, egg cartons, coffee cans, and soup cans.

• Assemble a collection of "prop boxes" for your child's imaginary play. In one box have grocery store items and a cash register (see previous suggestion); in another, puppets for a puppet show. Some other prop box suggestions are: fireman or policeman, doctor or nurse, Indians and cowboys, a filling station. (3-8 yrs.)

• Save all the "stamps" that come in the mail with advertisements for magazine subscriptions. Give your child a wet sponge to dampen the stamps. Then let your child stick them on paper to make a picture or design. (3-7 yrs.)

• Save used out-of-date clothing, jewelry, shoes, and hats. Children love to dress up. They especially like big hats and frilly clothes, firemen's hats, construction workers' hats, and pins and badges with sayings on them. Lipbalm is a harmless lipstick for dress-up. (3-10 yrs.)

• Old Halloween costumes and masks (on sale after the holiday) make excellent dress-up clothes to be used all year round.

• Give your children some old stamp pads. You may be able to find discarded printers' letters. If you can't find the whole alphabet, try to find the letters of your children's names. Some stamps come with numbers and pictures, too. Give your children ink pads or paint, and let them create. (3-7 yrs.)

• Play pretend: house (wash doll clothes and hang them on a low line); store (save old food cartons); trip (pack bags, write tickets, arrange chairs). (3-8 yrs.)

Inside Fun

• Place a piece of paper over different textured objects such as a comb, coins, shells, or buttons. Have your child run a crayon over the objects and see what designs he or she can make. (4-8 yrs.)

• Staple a piece of carbon paper between two sheets of paper. Let your child draw a picture. Then you can reveal the duplicate "magic" image. (4-6 yrs.)

• After a finger painting dries, have your child use his or her imagination to find "hidden pictures" in the artwork. (3-8 yrs.)

• Cover one of your small child's old shirts with buttons or small bells. He or she will enjoy playing with the decorations on the shirt. Put your child in front of a mirror in order to see better. Caution: Make sure everything is sewn on securely and check periodically for loose parts. (1-2 yrs.)

• Small plastic containers with lids make rattles when filled with seeds or balls. (Make sure that you tape them shut.) When your child gets older, use for storing tiny toys. (1-2 yrs.)

• Have your child lie down on a large sheet of paper and trace around him or her. Let your child fill in the face and clothing, cut the picture out, and hang it up for display. (3-8 yrs.)

• Keep your little baker busy with an inexpensive set of cake decorating tools. Fill the tube with mashed potatoes dyed with food coloring instead of icing—it's cheaper and sugar-free. Your child can experiment with the different designs each attachment makes. When the fun is over, the artwork can be eaten. (4-10 yrs.)

• Paste a simple picture on a thin piece of cardboard and outline it with a paper hole punch. Next, dip one end of a piece of yarn into nail polish and let it dry. Your child can then sew in and out of the holes and outline the picture with a "needle and thread." (4-7 yrs.)

dyed macaroni necklace (food coloring is dye)

• Preserve your child's artwork by placing it between sheets of waxed paper and pressing it with a warm iron. Use this creation as a placemat. Fall leaves "sandwiched" in the same way make lovely window decorations. (3-8 yrs.)

• This is for those "Well, why not?" days. Fill your tub with barefoot kids of varying heights and squirt the tiles around the bath with shaving cream. The children can use this like finger paint to make faces, designs and interesting blobs on the tile. After the giggles subside, hose down kids and tiles. Both should be cleaner. (3-10 yrs.)

• For more inside fun ideas, see the "Craft Recipes" section.

Games (And How to Play Them), by Anne F. Rockwell. (New York: Crowell, Thomas Y., Co., 1979.) (preschool & up)

Games & Puzzles You Can Make Yourself, by Harvey Weiss. (New York: Crowell Thomas Y., Co., 1973.) (older child)

Outside Fun

• Children always enjoy running through low-hanging laundry on the line. Instead of taking the chance of seeing your clean wash on the ground, put sheets, lightweight blankets, or long pants on the line and let them run through this clothing on a day other than laundry day. Don't put anything on the line that could cause injury. Watch out for pants or a dress with a buckle. (2-6 yrs.)

• Bubbles everywhere—a hand eggbeater and some detergent in a bucket of water. Definitely an outdoor activity. (3-5 yrs.)

• On a smaller scale, a drop of detergent in a cup of water and a straw can make a lot of cascading bubbles, too, but please, *warn your child not to suck in.* (3-5 yrs.)

• Mix soap flakes and water and beat them with an eggbeater. They become fluffy and foamy and make good fingerpaints. Pictures show up better if you paint on colored paper. (2-8 yrs.)

• When the weather is warm, my daughter's playmate, Keir, enjoys "painting" trees, the patio, and the sidewalk with a pail of water and several wide brushes. (2-5 yrs.)

• Open your own "Sandbox Bakery" by filling jello custard molds with wet sand. Other cooking utensils are empty bleach bottles with the tops cut off, tin cans, old measuring cups, old silverware, or cups and pans. (3-7 yrs.)

• Dampen an empty spool of thread, rub soap on one end of the spool, and blow bubbles by blowing on the other end. Fun for outdoors or in the bathtub. (3-5 yrs.)

• Partially fill empty detergent or bleach bottles with sand or water, set up the "pins," and bowl. Make sure that the lids are screwed on tightly. This game has provided many hours of entertainment for my son and his friends. (4-10 yrs.)

• Caterpillar and ladybug races are a lot of fun. (5-10 yrs.)

• *Fence Weaving:* Using old scraps of cloth, rags, twine, string, yarn and construction paper, you can weave a chain-link fence into something that's, well, unique. Your older child will want something that looks organized, while your 18-month-old will just want to poke something through the fence. Provide plenty of material, and either direct each child to his or her own area of the fence or make it a group project. (18 mo.-10 yrs.)

Little Kid's Four Seasons Craft Book, by Jackie Vermeer. (New York: Taplinger Publishing Co., Inc., 1974.) (k-6 yrs.)

Great Big Box Book, by Flo Ann Norvell. (New York: Crowell, Thomas Y., Co., 1979.) (5-10 yrs.)

Great American Book of Sidewalk, Stoop, Dirt, Curb, and Alley Games, by Fred Ferretti. (New York: Taplinger Publishing Co., Inc., 1974.) (k-6 yrs.)

Exciting Things to Do with Nature Materials, by Judy Allen. (New York: Lippincott, J.B., Co., 1977.) (5-10 yrs.)

Oh No, It's Raining!

• To keep kids occupied on rainy days, give them the task of setting out containers to gather rainwater for houseplants.

• Whenever you find a trinket you think your child might enjoy, hide it away. Include a few edible goodies, and on some dreary rainy day you'll have a ready-made cure for the grumps.

• Cookie cutters and play dough are always fun.

• Create an indoor sandbox. Place rice or cornmeal in a large pan, put newspaper or plastic under and around the pan and your child can dig or play with small cars or trucks in this mini-sandbox. (Rice works better because it does not spoil like cornmeal.) (2-7 yrs.)

indoor sandbox (rice)

• Make a yarn ball. Tie old bits of yarn together and attach trinkets to the lengthening string. Keep winding the yarn into a ball and get it out on a rainy day. These can also make great party favors. (3-10 yrs.)

• Build and stack with a deck of cards. (7-10 yrs.)

• Decorate a large sheet of paper together in any way you want. Display it as a mural. (2-10 yrs.)

• Plastic hair rollers make good tunnels for small cars or can be used for stacking. (2-10 yrs.)

• To make a potato-toothpick erector set, dice up two or three potatoes in small chunks and your child can construct his own building by joining potato to toothpick to potato. It's a real favorite of my son's friend, Kevin. (4-10 yrs.)

• Dip the end of a piece of yarn into nail polish, let it dry, and then string beads, cheerios, or macaroni with the "needle and thread." (3-6 yrs.)

• Let your children color your grocery bags with magic markers. You won't have to worry about ink from the markers coming through onto the table, and they'll be very proud of the fancy trash bags they create for your kitchen. (3-6 yrs.)

• Play with your hose phone or string telephone. Instructions in the "To Make for In or Out" section.

• Tape children's specials from the television and save them for a rainy day. Your child won't mind if he or she sees *How the Grinch Stole Christmas* in July. He or she can even enjoy just listening to a program on a cassette. (4-10 yrs.)

• A "rainy day" break for Mom or Dad—Put a headset on your child and let him or her listen to records. Enjoy some quiet time while your child is busy and in one place. (4-10 yrs.)

• Your older child can weave everything in his room with a ball of string, yarn, or ribbon, and then play in the imaginary spider web. (7-10 yrs.)

• Take a rainy day walk outside with rubbers, raincoat, and umbrella or a "discovery" walk around the house.

• For more rainy day fun, use the "Craft Recipe" section.

• A tension rod between the door jambs serves as a ballet barre for your child. (5-10 yrs.)

• String buttons with needle and thread. (4-7 yrs.)

What To Do When "There's Nothing to Do:—601 Tested Play Ideas for Young Children, by Children's Hospital Medical Center. (New York: Delacorte Press, 1968.) (18 mo.-5 yrs.)

Rainy-Day Book, by Allen Schwartz, (New York: Trident Press, 1968.) (5-10 yrs.)

48 *more* helpful hints on:

Toys

Toy Selection

The following general classifications of toys by age groupings are based on the Toy Manufacturers of America booklet, *Choosing Toys for Children of All Ages.*

Under 18 months

rattles
nursery mobiles
soft animals
crib-gym exercisers
strings of big beads
picture blocks
nested boxes or cups
books with rhymes, pictures, jingles
push-pull toys
floating tub toys
musical toys

pounding toys
stacking toys
small light wagon
simple take-apart-and-assemble toys
cuddle toys

18 months-3 years

riding toy to straddle or wagon to get into

hobby horse

balls at least 1 1/4 inches wide

child-size play furniture

play appliances and utensils

simple dress-up clothes

blocks of different sizes and shapes

stuffed animals

dolls and doll furniture

puzzles with large pieces

take-apart-and-put-together toys with large parts

clay, modeling dough

large crayons

(PG) blackboard and chalk, and finger paints

simple musical instruments

3-6 years

puppets

storekeeping toys

toy phone and toy clock

housekeeping toys

farm, village and other community play sets

small trucks, cars, planes, boats

easy construction sets

beginner plastic model kits

(PG) blackboard and chalk

party favors

puzzles

large crayons and paper

(PG) marbles

books

records

paste, blunt scissors

picture books and simple story line books

peg boards, large pegs and beads

non-toxic paints, opaque water colors, large brushes, easels

stacking and interlocking blocks

6-9 years

board games

tabletop sports games

fashion dolls

doll houses

paper dolls

toy typewriter

printing sets

racing cars

construction sets

take-apart-and-put-together toys with small parts

(PG) electric trains

(PG) science sets

tops

(PG) marbles

handicrafts

skates

pogo sticks

more advanced books

(PG) carpentry tools

9-12 years

(PG) advanced model kits

make-up and good grooming sets

(PG) chemistry and other science sets

(PG) trains and auto race sets

advanced construction sets

marionettes

jigsaw puzzles

card games

handicrafts

electronic computer based toys

(PG): parental guidance is recommended

- For pamphlets and more information write:
    Toy Manufacturers of America, Inc.
    200 Fifth Ave.
    New York, New York 10010
    (212) 675-1141

- It's very important that your infant receive plenty of stimulation, but expensive toys aren't necessary. Look at household objects through your little one's eyes, and you'll see toys everywhere: paper bags, plastic utensils, clean cloth of different textures, pots and pans, wooden spoons (almost anything with no small pieces or sharp edges that can harm your child.) And remember that the best toy of all is a parent!

- When shopping for baby toys, make a stop at the pet store; many of the noisy, squeaky items that animals love are equally delightful to little people.

- Be sure to buy toys that are bigger than your child's fist. This will help protect him or her from swallowing or choking on small toys.

• Select stuffed animals with embroidered eyes. Button-type eyes can be pulled off and swallowed.

• Garage and house sales are great places to find children's toys in good condition and at a fraction of the cost in the store. Many nursery schools and parents organizations sponsor sales, too. Check for ads in local papers.

• A friend suggests that if you see a display in a store that your child might enjoy, leave your name and number with the department manager. Have them call you when they're ready to discard the display.

• It seems that a child always enjoys a toy more at a friend's house. Arrange a toy swap with neighbors. Tape your name on your toys and exchange them with friends. When you child tires of the toy, return to its owner.

• Don't keep all of your children's toys out, with the exception of those they play with frequently. By rotating the supplies of toys, they will have renewed interest in toys they don't play with constantly.

• Save your baby's outgrown clothing and underwear. When your child is older, these tiny things can be used to dress dolls. (4-8 yrs.)

• A geodesic dome to climb on is a wonderful toy that a child will enjoy for many years. Cover it with an old sheet to make a tent. (3-10 yrs.)

Additional reading
Choosing Toys for Children from Birth to Five, by Barbara Kaban. (New York: Schocken Books, Inc., 1979.)

Care and Fixin'

• Remove magic marker or pen marks from toys with nail polish remover.

• Are you missing a piece to your toy or game? Is a piece broken? Write to the manufacturer for a replacement parts price list.

• Use vaseline to lubricate your child's toys. It will get the wheels moving and eliminate squeaks in a tricycle. Another plus is that it's inexpensive and non-toxic.

• A toy box lid is dangerous if it falls onto your child. Either remove it completely, or put a magnetic cabinet fastener on the wall and one one the outside of the lid. Every time the lid is opened, it will stay open.

• Inflatable toys seem always to be sprouting holes! Find the hole by placing it in water and looking for air bubbles. Be sure to mark around the hole so you'll be able to locate it easily and repair it later. When the surface is dry, patch the hole with a vinyl sealer from the hardware store.

• Cover the pages in activity books (books with puzzles, games, connect the dots pictures, and mazes) with clear plastic adhesive. If you supply your child with grease pencils, the pages can be used over and over.

• If you put a picture on side one of your child's record, he or she can use it to guess the title. This will aid in selection and help decide which side to play first.

To Make For In and Out

• *Fishing Pole:* Put a magnet on one end of a string and attach the other end to a dowel rod or stick. Cut familiar pictures out of magazines or cut fish shapes from a plastic gallon milk jug. Put a paper clip on the "fish," place them in a box or bucket and let your child fish. (2-7 yrs.)

• *Paper Bag Kite:* Attach a piece of yarn to both sides of the open end of a brown paper lunch bag and glue crepe paper streamers to the bottom of the bag. As your child runs, the bag will "catch" the air and fly along behind him or her. (2-7 yrs.)

- *Paper Bag Blocks:* Fill paper grocery store bags with newspaper and tape them shut. Your child can use these to build with or jump on. Other things around the house to use for building are tin can blocks, hair rollers, or small cardboard boxes. (2-8 yrs.)

- *Giant Checkers Game:* Save plastic lids from margarine tubs or coffee cans and paint them red and black. Draw a checkerboard with chalk on the patio, sidewalk or basement floor. (8-10 yrs.)

- *Train:* Join several shoe boxes with cord. Let your child fill the train with stuffed animals and pull them around for a train ride. (2-6 yrs.)

- *Stilts:* For a small child, two coffee cans will do. Poke holes in each side and insert a loop of cord that will reach his or her hands. Your child will stand on the cans, hold them tightly to his or her feet with the cords, and clomp around thrilled to be the tallest kid on the block. (3-10 yrs.)

- *Playhouse or Puppet Theater:* Go to the warehouse of a music store and ask for an empty piano box. These are much sturdier than discarded refrigerator boxes. Use the box for a playhouse or puppet theater. Lots of room for small kids. (3-10 yrs.)

- *Playhouse:* Wrap a wide sheet of plastic around three trees that are close together. Leave enough room between the ground and the plastic so the children can get into and out of the house. You may also use butcher paper to wrap around the trees so the children can decorate their house freely with paint. Important: Remind them that paper can tear. (3-10 yrs.)

• *Tunnel:* Lean a section of rain gutter on an outside step or a railing. Your child can slide his cars down the imaginary tunnel. (2-6 yrs.)

• *Hose Phone:* Cut the nozzle and screw end off of an old garden hose. Put a child on either end and let them talk to each other. If you want to be fancy, tape a funnel onto each end. Two tin cans joined with a piece of string also make a telephone. (4-10 yrs.)

• *Sled:* Your child's old plastic bathtub makes an excellent sled. It won't go too fast and the sides keep the child from falling. (2-7 yrs.)

• *Tire Swing:* Cut away the tread 3/4 of the way around a tire. Turn the tire inside out and add ropes. Make sure you use nylon rope. It's stronger and won't rot. (2-10 yrs.)

• *A Secret Hiding Place:* Children enjoy being in quiet, secret hiding places. Check out a salvage yard and see if they have old tires or some concrete pipe that you can set into the ground; or metal barrels to anchor in place, and use for tunnels. Many of these items are free. Other secret spots are tree houses, tents, or the area under the porch. (2-10 yrs.)

• *Sandbox:* Use your child's outgrown plastic wading pool for a sandbox. Punch holes in the bottom for drainage, and place in the ground.

For your young child
Toys to Make & Ride, by C.J. MacGinley. (New York: Harcourt Brace Jovanovich, Inc., 1977.) (3-5 yrs.)

Milk Carton Blocks, by Bernie Zubrowski. (Boston: Little, Brown & Co., 1979.) (2-10 yrs.)

For young or old
Toymaking, Children's Furniture Simplified, by Donald Brann. (Directions Simplified, 1977.)

Soft Toys, by C.J. MacGinley. (New York: Harcourt Brace Jovanovich, Inc., 1977.) (2-10 yrs.)

For older kids
Steve Caney's Toy Book, by Steven Caney. (New York: Workman Publishing Co., Inc., 1972.) (5-10 yrs.)

Building with Tires, Early Education Study, by Terry d'Eugenio. (Cambridge, Mass., 1971.)

Build Your Own Plaground! A Source Book of Play Sculptures, by Jeremy Joan Hewes. (Boston: Houghton Mifflin Co., 1974.)

Storage

• Save large coffee cans, large plastic containers, ice cream containers, (free from the ice cream store) and small boxes. Cover them with contact paper and a picture of what should be stored inside. You may have containers for small cars and trucks, another for pretend food, or another for farm animals. All your child's small things will be together. Not only does this help you when your child requests a certain toy, but at clean up time you and your child can practice categorizing each item.

• Laundry baskets make excellent toy boxes. Children can carry them around, and clean-up time is much easier since you can cart the basket to the mess.

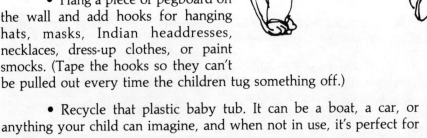

• Ryan, my son's friend, has such a collection of Lego Building Blocks that he stores them in a large fishing tackle box. The box is big enough for all his blocks, and the sections make it simple to divide them up by sizes and shapes.

• A child's shoe bag can be hung up in the playroom and used for storing stuffed animals, action figures, or small dolls.

• Hang a piece of pegboard on the wall and add hooks for hanging hats, masks, Indian headdresses, necklaces, dress-up clothes, or paint smocks. (Tape the hooks so they can't be pulled out every time the children tug something off.)

• Recycle that plastic baby tub. It can be a boat, a car, or anything your child can imagine, and when not in use, it's perfect for storing toys.

• After you child has outgrown the bassinet, use it for a toy box.

• Horizontal storage is better than vertical. Small items can become lost and forgotten in the bottom of big boxes.

• A bookshelf is an excellent "toy chest." Everything is visible, and there are no lids to fall on little ones.

• Paint the storage shelves in your child's room different colors. Color code all toys, then your child will know what toy goes on which shelf when it's time to clean up.

• Place cup hooks on a shelf, then hang baskets or buckets of small objects above larger items on the shelf below.

• Turn cardboard boxes on their sides and cover them with contact paper. These make wonderful bookshelves or places to store records.

• Store your child's view-master slides in a round plastic deli or margarine tub. This will keep them all together and bend-free.

• Missing puzzle pieces? Solution: Place the pieces in zip-lock bags. Be sure to label the bag so you know what puzzle it belongs to.

• One of my friend's best garage sale finds was an old piano bench. It made a great work table for her children since it was just the right height, and under the lid was storage for colors, crayons, and papers.

• Save room on your bookshelf for your child's favorite books.

117 *more* helpful hints on:

Special Times

Happy Birthday

Invites and Thank-yous
• Inflate balloons and write the date, time, and location of the party on them. After they're dry, let the air out, enclose each in an envelope and mail. Be sure to include directions about inflating them in the envelope.

• Enclose a self-addressed, stamped envelope with a birthday invitation. Your guest can RSVP and your child will receive mail addressed to him or her.

• Creative thank-you notes can be written on the back of the wrapping paper that the gift came in. Your child might even want to cut out pictures from the wrapping paper and paste them on paper to make thank-you notes. (3-10 yrs.)

• Make a thank-you note with a photo of the guest at the party. The parents will appreciate it.

• To cut down on the number at a birthday party, limit your child to one guest for each year old, i.e. 3 guests for your child's third birthday.

• Mothers of the guests go to a lot of trouble selecting a gift for the party. Why not remember them by sending a small inexpensive gift home for the mother with a thank-you note attached?

Get Organized
• Many parents suggest providing your family with a wish box. Have family members place their gift requests inside. You'll have an idea of what to get them for birthday presents or will have suggestions for friends and relatives when they ask.

• You've gone to a lot of trouble preparing for your child's party. Make sure you enjoy it, too. Hire a babysitter or two to help out. They may even be talented and can put on a puppet show or a magic show.

• Save your breath! Use a bicycle pump to blow up the balloons for the party.

• Double-faced carpet tape on the bottom of bowls save a lot of accidental spills.

• Stand the birthday candles in a marshmallow or gumdrop so no wax will spill on the cake.

• An ironing board at its lowest position makes a handy extra table when a large group is eating at your house. Or if you have plenty of eating space, (but not much serving space), use it as a buffet.

• Be sure to have a lot of film on hand for photos. Take a group picture of all the guests so your child will have a record of all those in attendance to place in the birthday scrapbook. Identify each guest by name. (For more records of special events, see the "Memories" section.)

• Clean-up after a party is much easier if you give each guest a bag and announce that you have one more prize for the person who picks up the most ribbons and paper.

Themes
• Parties are more fun to have or plan if you pick a theme. Discuss it with your children and let them choose something they like, Example: For a "Pirate Party" provide the children with pirate hats, bandanas, and chocolate candy wrapped in gold paper to resemble doubloons. Have a treasure hunt. Hide a chest of pennies and have the children search for it. Play musical islands instead of musical chairs by placing paper islands on the ground for the children to step on.

• *Birthday Party Themes:*

Trains and planes	Cowboys and Indians
Mother Goose	Sports
Favorite doll—each kid brings one for the party	Fairy Tales
	Cartoons
Seasons	Dinosaurs
Circus	Outer Space
Beach Party	

• Six to ten-year-olds know what kind of party they want. Let them help you plan it and act as host or hostess during it.

• *Party Excuse:* A former teaching colleague, Arlene, shares one of her family's favorites. Celebrate your child's half birthday. Ice only half a cake, sing only half a birthday song, celebrate for only half an hour, spend only half as much for a small gift, use half candles. Your child will really enjoy the party and so will you. (1-10 yrs.)

Food
• Fill flat-bottomed ice cream cones half-full with cake batter. Place on a cookie sheet and bake in the oven. Add icing, sprinkle

If you serve a meal, keep it simple! Kids would rather play than eat. Try peanut butter & jelly, hot dogs, hamburgers, or pizza, and, of course, potato chips.

powdered sugar or top with cream cheese icing. (Softened cream cheese mixed with honey).

• Prepare balls of ice cream and freeze ahead of time. When it's time to serve cake and ice cream, you'll be fast and fair to all.

• Instead of the regular cake and ice cream, have an ice cream smorgasbord. Put out all the kinds of toppings—nuts, sauces, fruit, etc., and let the children make their own creation.

• Fill an empty cardboard tube with goodies, tape the ends shut, and give it to your guests.

• Everyone likes peanut butter and jelly sandwiches. Use cookie cutters to cut their favorite into different shapes. Find cookie cutters that fit the theme of your party, if possible.

Is Everybody Happy?
• Plan more activities than you think you have time for. You'd be surprised at how fast games go.

• Here's an activity that can continue throughout the party; Place instructions on paper inside balloons. Some ideas are: sing, pretend to be a football player, dance, do some exercises, etc. Whenever someone's balloon breaks, they have to perform according to the instruction. (3-10 yrs.)

• Pin the tail on the donkey is a standard party game. Adapt it to fit the theme of your party, i.e., pin the tail on the dinosaur, on the elephant, etc. Hint: Use tape instead of pins and you will save your walls. (3-10 yrs.)

• Piñatas can be made very simply by placing goodies in a paper grocery bag and tying it to a tree. Each child has a turn to take a whack, blindfolded, until it breaks and the toys are scattered. (3-10 yrs.)

• Hide prizes around the house and let the guests have a treasure hunt. Important: Take all the prizes to a central location and divide them up *equally*. (3-10 yrs.)

• Party favors and prizes are easily misplaced. Provide each guest with a paper lunch bag decorated by your child. This way, the kids will each have a place to keep party favors. Make sure you place the guest's name on the bag to avoid arguments. (3-10 yrs.)

• Steve, father of Daniel and Benjamin, learns some simple magic tricks, dresses up, and performs for his children's birthday parties. He says they never notice his lack of expertise.

• If you have an older brother or sister in the family, let the child help out by putting on a puppet show with the younger children.

• Many people hire clowns for their parties for entertainment. If you don't want to go to that expense, check out a child's movie from the library. It's free, and the children will enjoy the movie. (3-10 yrs.)

write name BIG, on both sides

Let each child decorate his own "goodie bag"— and have a special place for all of them.

• An even better entertainer is a video recording of a children's television special such as *Puff the Magic Dragon*. This will not only entertain your party guests, but can be used again by your children for any occasion. This film was a real success at our friend, Kevin's birthday party. (3-8 yrs.)

• Your child has a winter birthday, and you can't bear the thought of having so many children indoors! Why not take the children somewhere as a group? Many places offer special parties for children. Go to a fast food restaurant, an ice skating or roller skating rink, a hockey game, or a bowling alley. (5-10 yrs.)

• Take an empty shopping bag along when you're the chaperone on a group birthday party. You're sure to turn into the keeper of sweaters, mittens, hats, or any other little item that interferes with their enjoyment.

Other Party Activities
• *Bag Plays:* Divide guests into equal groups. Provide each group with a lunch bag filled with little things you find around the house. Each group must make up a play using each item in the bag. After all the plays have been given, trade bags among the groups and let them create new plays. (6-10 yrs.)

• *Scavenger Hunt:* Divide the guests into equal groups. Give each group the same list of items. Assign them different streets or territories. Send them out into the neighborhood to gather the items, only one per house or apartment. The team that gathers all the items first, wins. This can be done with things from nature on a picnic or club hike. (7-10 yrs.)

• *Bike Trip:* Have kids meet you at a particular point with their bikes. Bring refreshments and bike to a special spot for a birthday picnic. (9-10 yrs.)

Wrap It Up
• Use a ball of yarn to tie up gifts. It's much cheaper than ribbon and looks just as nice.

• Recycle undamaged wrapping paper and crinkle-free ribbons from gifts you receive.

• Place the instructions for the location of a gift inside a box and have the child search for the hiding place.

• My son's friend, Matthew, is fascinated by railroads and anything to do with trains. The birthday gifts he gives are wrapped in

WRAPS: Brown paper, butcher paper, computer paper, comic strips, magazines, old phone book pages, cloth scraps. DECORATE with: flowers, balloons, stick-ons, yarn dipped in glue, cut-out pictures, buttons, old paintings, & imagination.

his original artwork—showing trains and tracks, of course. Matthew's present is always opened carefully, and the wrapping paper is held up and admired. The gift stays behind, but Matthew likes to take the artwork home again. Your child might enjoy making original wrapping paper, too.

• A good slumber party gift is a pillowcase embroidered with the host's name and birthdate.

• Keep a drawer in your house reserved for gifts for future party invites. Fill it with birthday party gifts you find on sale or with duplicate gifts your child has received. You'll be ready on short notice. Be sure to store these items where your own children won't make a delightful discovery.

For further party information
Party Plans for Tots, by Kate Harris. (Chicago: Follett Publishing Co., 1967.)

For an older child
So You Want to Plan A Birthday Party!, by Catherine Durkin. (New York: Atheneum Pubs., 1980.)

• For books to read to your child, see "About Birthdays" in the "Books to Read Along With Children" section.

Valentine's Day

• An original Valentine card is a "thumbprint heart card." Have your child dip his thumb into paint or into an ink pad and make two thumbprints, touching in the shape of the letter V. (3-10 yrs.)

• Make the oven art dough recipe in the "Craft Recipes" section, roll it out and cut out heart shapes with a cookie cutter. Before baking, have your child "draw" a Valentine message with a toothpick or orange stick. When the hearts are cool, they can be painted red and passed out to friends as gifts. (*Not* edible) (4-10 yrs.)

• Draw and decorate a heart shape on a piece of cardboard. Cut out the heart shape and then cut into pieces to make a puzzle. Put it into an envelope for a different Valentine's Day greeting for a friend. (4-8 yrs.)

• An old-fashioned touch for a Valentine greeting is a cut-out picture or heart made from red paper and glued to a paper doily. (3-7 yrs.)

• Valentine-shaped cinnamon toast is a big treat at breakfast.

• For lunch or snack time, cut out heart shapes from slices of bread. Spread on strawberry jam and enjoy!

For age 6-10 yrs
Blue Valentine, by Gwen Shultz. (New York: Morrow, William & Co., Inc., 1979.)

Easter

• Before Easter, start to make a collection of egg shells by blowing out the egg before you use it. (Egg-blowing instructions below). By the time Easter arrives, you'll have quite a few hollow eggs to color and no wasted eggs after the holiday.

• To blow out eggs, make a small hole in one end of the egg with a sharp object. Make another hole on the other end, a little larger. Insert a toothpick in the larger hole and break the yolk. Blow hard through the small hole to empty the shell. Rinse the shell and save.

• *Egg Decorations:* Cut comic-strip characters or creatures from Easter ads and glue them with white glue to colored eggs.

The night before, put out carrots for the bunny.

Striped Eggs! Put rubber bands around the dyed eggs before they dry.

Dribble candle wax for a pretty effect.

Drop dye onto the egg with an eye-dropper for a pastel colored blended effect.

For a rainbow effect, scribble on a *hard boiled* egg using different colors. Then, cover the entire egg with black crayon. Next, scrape off the black in a pattern using a coin or spoon. Remember: Don't attempt to do this on a hollow egg, use hard boiled ones. (3-10 yrs.)

• It seems a shame to waste extra egg dye. Use old eyedroppers to dribble the color onto paper towels. They will blend together to make lovely patterns. When dry, the child can use them for placemats or doilies. (3-7 yrs.)

• Crushed egg shells, when glued, make nice collages. (2-8 yrs.)

• To make an Easter egg hunt fair for the younger children, color the eggs in only two colors. Designate one color for the younger children and hide them in easy-to-find places. Hide the other color eggs in difficult places for the older children. This way everyone gets a chance to hunt and gather a lot of eggs and the little ones will enjoy a sense of accomplishment.

• Save the crafts your children make at school (bunnies, chicks, and Easter baskets). Identify with the name of your children and the year and save for future Easters. When they're older, they'll be proud to see the things they made, and you'll have plenty of Easter decorations.

For more hints:
Easter Eggs for Everyone, by Evelyn Coskey. (Nashville, TN: Abingdon Press, 1973.)

Purim
• *Purim Rattle:* Place beans or seeds inside a small plastic foam meat tray. Glue a second tray of the same size on top. When the glue is dry, sew the edges together with a large needle threaded with yarn; then paint. (4-10 yrs.)

• *Royal Crown:* Cut a length of lightweight cardboard, about 5" wide, to fit around your child's head. Staple the ends together and scallop a design around the top. Cover with aluminum foil and decorate with glitter. (3-10 yrs.)

• Use paper bags to make masks of the Purim characters. (See the instructions for paper bag masks.) (2-10 yrs.)

Additional suggestions
My Very Own Megillah, by Judyth Saypol. (Silver Spring, MD: Kar-Ben Copies, 1976.) (4-10 yrs.)

Halloween
• When passing out Halloween goodies, remove the top portion of your screen door to save reaching around the door to hand out treats.

• Many young children are frightened by Halloween masks. To keep your children from feeling left out of the fun, paint their faces with water soluble make-up. Most toy stores carry this product, and it is safer than a mask because vision isn't impaired.

• A child's sleeper can be the basis for a Halloween costume. Add big ears and a fluffy tail to make a bunny.

• Warts and scars? Yes, that's what your child wants to look like. Purchase some moleskin in a drugstore. It's self-adhesive, inexpensive, and can be cut out to the desired shape, painted, and applied.

• Put reflector tape on your child's Halloween costume, so he or she can be easily seen outside at night.

• Alternatives to candy for Halloween: Raisins, sugarless gum, balloons, little toys, nickels, or several pennies.

• Instead of carving just a pumpkin, let your child carve other fruits and vegetables such as apples, carrots, potatoes, or spaghetti squash. (4-10 yrs.)

• At a Halloween party you can "pin the tail on the black cat;" make bean bags and toss them into a cardboard pumpkin's mouth; or fish for spiders and bats. (See instructions for making a fishing pole.) (2-7 yrs.)

More ideas

Star Trek, the Motion Picture, Make-Your-Own Costume Book, by Lynn Schnurnberger. (New York: Pocket Books, Inc., 1979.) (6-10 yrs.)

Easy Costumes You Don't Have to Sew, by Goldie Chernoff. (New York: Four Winds Press, 1975.) (1-7 yrs.)

Thanksgiving

• Your child can make the Thanksgiving tablecloth with a large sheet of paper or an old tablecloth. Decorate the tablecloth with magic markers and pictures of pilgrims, or a turkey. Or your child can draw on the "placemats" and put each guest's name on the tablecloth. (4-10 yrs.)

• Design Thanksgiving Day greeting cards. Fold a sheet of paper in half; glue pictures or draw a Thanksgiving scene on the front of the card; and place a greeting inside. A "handprint turkey" (below) also makes a nice card decoration. (3-10 yrs.)

hand-print turkey; point in features, glue on feathers.

• Make a turkey print using your child's hand. (2-7 yrs.)

Additional reading:
Things To Make and Do for Thanksgiving, by Lorinda Cauley. (New York: Watts, Franklin, Inc., 1977.)

Hanukkah

• Make a dreidel from an old top painted with acrylic paints. When it is dry, draw on one of the Hebrew letters on each of the four sides. (4-10 yrs.)

Jewish and Christian kids can share in each other's holidays.

• Use the Oven Art recipe in the "Craft Recipes" section to make a Star of David, a lion, dreidel, and candles with Hanukkah cookie cutters. (These are available at department stores and Hebrew bookstores.) (4-10 yrs.)

These same Hanukkah cookie cutters can be used to cut shapes from sponges. Dip the shapes in paint to make sponge paints for pictures or for wrapping paper. (3-10 yrs.)

• Also make printed wrapping paper with the end of a spool of thread dipped into paint to make "latkes," or paper clips dipped and arranged to form the Star of David. (4-10 yrs.)

• *Hanukkah Mobile:* Use construction paper to cut out shapes of things associated with Hanukkah such as dreidels, latkes, candles, Menorahs, or shields and attach them with different lengths of string to a wire clothes hanger. (3-10 yrs.)

• Nine empty juice cans can be used to make a Menorah. Cover each can with a piece of construction paper, then paint a Hanukkah character or design on each can. Fill the cans with plaster of Paris; when the plaster is almost set; insert a candle to form a hole. (Move the candle around a little to make the hole slightly larger.) Remove the candle until the plaster is completely dry. (4-10 yrs.)

• To make Hanukkah greeting cards, cut out two triangles and use them to form a Star of David. Paste these on a sheet of constrution paper that has been folded in half. Put your message inside the card. (2-10 yrs.)

For all ages
Let's Celebrate, by Ruth Esrig Brinn. (Silver Spring, MD: Kar-Ben Copies, 1977.)

Power of Light: Eight Stories for Hanukkah, by Isaac B. Singer. (New York: Farrar Books, 1980.) (7-10 yrs.)

Christmas
• Save old Christmas cards. When your child becomes too unbearably eager for the season to begin, last year's cards can be cut up to make deocrations, ornaments, bookmarks, or placemats. (Cover with clear adhesive paper, or press with a warm iron between two sheets of waxeu paper to make placemats.) (3-10 yrs.)

• Start the countdown to Christmas by interlocking strips of paper to form a chain. Have a circle for each day before Christmas and tear one off each day. (3-7 yrs.)

• Another way to wait for Christmas is to purchase a child's Advent calendar. Starting on December 1, your child can look forward to opening a window each day and seeing the hidden scene. This is fun and a good way to learn numbers while learning about the things associated with Christmas. If you are careful not to tear off the numbered windows, you can use the calendar year after year. (3-7 yrs.)

• Create your own Advent wreath. Use a small pie tin and stand four small candles in it. Stabilize them with wax and decorate with greens. (3-8 yrs.)

• After Thanksgiving, get a notebook (or staple sheets of construction paper together to make a book). Each person should have a page of his or her own to enter the things he or she would like for Christmas. On the reverse side of each person's sheet, include other information that will help in gift selection such as clothing size or favorite color.

• Save all the trinkets you get in cereal boxes or from any free offers and use them as stocking stuffers.

• If you have several small children who cannot read, wrap each child's gifts in different colored wrapping paper. This will save you time labeling the gifts.

• Children receive so many gifts, not only from Santa, but from friends and relatives too, that they are overwhelmed. Some gifts are ignored, some only played with occasionally. Take some of these least-liked toys and put them away. Bring out on a rainy day or have a summer Christmas, and see how popular the gifts become.

• During the after-Christmas sales, let your child pick out an ornament for next year's tree. Before you pack it away, put your child's name on it. By the time he or she has a personal tree, there'll be plenty of ornaments on hand. (3-10 yrs.)

• Here's how your children can make decorations to hang on the tree:

1. A paper cup can be inverted, decorated with fabric scraps, buttons, etc., and your bell can be hung with a piece of yarn on the tree.

2. Pine cones can be dipped in glue, covered with glitter, and hung on the tree.

3. Make paper snowflakes.

4. Paint a face on a bottle cork, glue on paper wings, put a screw eye on the top, and you are ready to hang the angel on your tree.

5. With a parent's help, grate pieces of broken crayons, place them between pieces of waxed paper, and press this with a warm iron for a "stained glass window."

6. String popcorn and cranberries together with needle and thread.

7. Draw Christmas pictures, mount them on construction paper, use a paper punch to make a hole, and hang them on the tree. Parents can date and save these mementos.

8. Trace or paint inside Christmas stencils—the kind you use with spray snow. Make a picture or cut them out and make a Christmas mobile.

9. Make your own wrapping paper. Parents can paint the palms of a child's hands and make handprints on plain paper. For designs, use a carved carrot or a potato dipped in paint.

10. Make ornaments with the modeling dough recipe in the "Craft Recipes" section.

• Everyone really enjoys decorating the Christmas tree, but helping take it down is another story. To solve this, have the children open all but one of their gifts. This gift can be unwrapped only when the tree is gone and everything is put away.

• Put on your brightest lipstick and leave a kiss from Santa on your child's cheek—a favorite discovery at our house on Christmas morning.

• A large pair of boots dipped in soot and "walked across" the floor makes Santa's footprints from the fireplace to the tree or cookie plate.

Other Christmas ideas
Christmas Crafts, Things to Make the 24 Days Before Christmas, by Carolyn Meyer. (New York: Harper & Row Pubs., Inc., 1974.) (7-10 yrs.)

For general holiday craft books
Let's Celebrate; Holiday Decorations You Can Make, by Peggy Parish. (New York: Morrow, William & Co., Inc., 1976.) (3-5 yrs.)

For the older child
Pumpkin In A Pear Tree: Creative Ideas for Twelve Months of Holiday Fun, by Ann Cole. (Boston: Little, Brown & Co., 1976.) (5-10 yrs.)

Gifts With a Personal Touch
• Each month of the coming year take a picture of your child doing something typical for the month. For example, flying a kite in March, in a Halloween costume in October, at the family dinner at Thanksgiving, your child's birthday, etc. Have these pictures enlarged and attach to a calendar for the coming year. Grandma and Grandpa will love their personalized gift.

• Another easy gift for a child to give is one in the form of an I.O.U. Label strips of paper, "Coupon: Redeemable on Command."

Write what the coupon is good for, or have the child draw a picture of the chore he or she will do, such as helping to clear the table, taking out the trash, or helping to wash the car. This idea can be used for Mother's or Father's Day, and for birthdays. Parents can use the same idea for a child's birthday or just to do something special. (4-10 yrs.)

• Make a collage of your child's artwork, frame it, and give it to grandparents as gifts.

• Have your child place his or her hands in poster paint, and print them on poster paper. Paint the child's name and the date underneath, and when the paint is dry, frame it. (1-10 yrs.)

• For something more elaborate, make a pattern of both your child's hands, trace onto fabric, and appliqué this to a rectangular piece of fabric. Embroider the child's name and the date below. Either stretch this across a frame or place it into a frame. (1-10 yrs.)

• Handprints can also be made in clay or plaster of Paris. Make sure you write down the name and date before it hardens. (1-10 yrs.)

• Silhouettes of your children make excellent gifts. Have them done or do them yourself.

• Collect photos of your children and arrange in a frame with matting cut to contain many photos. This makes a nice gift or a keep-sake for parents.

• If you prefer, purchase a small photo album and fill it with photos of your family. Favorite relatives will always have the album handy to show around.

• Put photos of your children inside a small hinged jewelry box, stand it on its side, and you have a double-picture frame.

• Cut out pictures of your children from duplicate photos, attach them to stationery to make personalized writing paper. Friends and relatives enjoy receiving these letters, and you have used otherwise extra photos.

• After a visit, have your children create a bread-and-butter note. They can draw pictures of the good times they had while visiting, or even write a poem to go along with the pictures. Hosts will enjoy receiving a different thank-you note. (4-10 yrs.)

Memories
• Save the newspaper from the day your child was born, and put it in a scrapbook.

• Keep a record of "oops," not just accomplishments.

• We tape our children's voices frequently. Even now, my son enjoys hearing himself (at a younger age) coo, giggle, sing, and recite.

• In addition to saving your child's first pair of shoes, save one of the very tiny first outfits to show your child how very small he or she was.

• Begin at the beginning—when your child is born or is a year old—and encourage the custom of buying a special book for each birthday celebrated. As your child gets older, shop together for the book. Consider it a library of his or her very own, a reflection of your child's interests over the years. (Be sure to record the birthday date *and* day of the week inside.)

• Take your movie camera with you wherever you go—not just on vacations. Before you film, make a sign that tells the date and where you are. Hold this up and film it first. It is an easy way to remember where you were and when.

• Purchase a photo album and fill it with photos of your child. During the first year, babies change and grow so fast, you should include a picture of your child for each month. Next to the picture include height, weight, accomplishments. After the first year, take an annual photo. Your child will enjoy going through this book, looking at the photos and seeing when he or she walked, crawled, spoke the first words, who came to birthday parties, and it will remind the parents of things they may have otherwise forgotten.

• Keep a large box with a lid for each child. Use it to collect their best pieces of artwork and identify with title and date. Parent and child can go through this box when the child is older.

• Many parents we know keep a notebook handy to jot down accomplishments as they happen.

• A very busy parent hangs an extra calendar in each child's bedroom to keep a separate record of important things in their lives. The calendar is easily accessible; entries are already dated; and it is a good way to teach days of the week, months, and numbers, too.

• After your child starts to talk, keep a notebook with a record of special words your toddler may have for certain objects or persons. Keep track of the funny things that have been said, too. Date the entries. My son once asked my suspender-wearing father-in-law why he wore his seat belt all the time.

• After a visit to a relative's house, a trip to the zoo, or the museum, give your child several sheets of paper stapled together like a booklet to draw pictures about what he or she did. After it's finished, sit down with your child and he or she can dictate the corresponding story to you! (3-7 yrs.)

• Have separate envelopes for each child and fill these envelopes with photos that would be special; for example, pictures of friends, pets, or memorable occasions. Give each child the envelope to look through periodically and to have as a keepsake when he or she becomes an adult.

• Vacation memories: If you've been to the beach, fill a pie tin or box lid with plaster, and let your child stick in shells, rocks, etc., that he or she has collected. (2-10 yrs.)

90 *more* helpful hints on:

Traveling

Things You Should Always Have in the Car

Towel (to cover a hot car seat in the summer)

A diaper or two

Moist towelettes

A box of tissues

Flashlight

Extra change for meters or phone calls

First Aid Kit

Stroller

A sheet of oilcloth for impromptu picnics

Activity toys for an occasional break on a long trip

An air-tight container with non-perishable foods such as raisins, cheerios, crackers.

A portable potty chair (You can't always find a bathroom when you want it.)

Small cans of fruit juice

A collapsible cup for water fountain drinks

An insulated ice chest for perishables

A litter bag or wastebasket

Some Pointers

• Mount your directions or destination on the windshield visor. They will always be within reach, and you won't have to take your eyes off the road to search for them.

• It's possible to purchase sample-sized portions of toothpaste, soap, deodorant, shampoo, and other toiletries (or you may receive these free samples in the mail). Rather than use them at home, keep them in a special small suitcase. If you have to pack in a hurry, you'll have everything you need at hand.

• For efficient packing, make up notecards that list the packing necessities for each family member. For example, for baby you'd list diapers, formula, pajamas, etc. Tape each person's list inside his or her closet. Be sure to make a notecard for bathroom needs, too, and if you plan to camp or rent a house at the beach, have a kitchen notecard made up and taped to the inside of a cabinet. Update these cards as your family's needs change.

• Save the plastic binders on loaves of bread and use them to hang up hand-washed articles. They take up much less space than clothespins.

• When purchasing a car seat for your infant, choose one that has a reclining position in addition to the upright position. Your child can nap comfortably with his or her feet resting on a propped-up suitcase.

• Make the switch to disposable diapers *before* the trip. Some children may have an allergic reaction to certain brands of disposable diapers, so it's wise to discover this *before* taking a trip.

• Pack the diapers in an extra suitcase. As you use the diapers, you'll have an empty suitcase for souvenirs and gifts.

• Prevent leaks. Place bottles of baby oil, shampoo, etc., in plastic bags before you pack them.

• A portable crib, playpen, or bassinet can serve as a bed. They take up more room than an inflatable pool, but they're safer if your child is at the exploratory stage.

• The best time for long trips is when your child is under six months of age. Take advantage of those long naps a small child requires.

Inflatable pillows are great— buy at a camping store.

• With older children, if you have a choice, travel during nap-time or in the evening. We've learned from our frequent out-of-state visits to leave about an hour or two before nap or bedtime. Then, just about the time the children are getting fussy, they fall asleep. This makes the trip faster for the child and so much more relaxing for us. Night-time or pre-dawn travel is even better.

• Staying overnight? Take your child's favorite stuffed animal or blanket along. It's a familiar and comforting sight.

• An old attaché case makes a good child's suitcase.

• Sharing a suitcase with your child? Put your child's clothing on top so they'll be easy to reach.

• When packing, put outfits together instead of all the pants in one stack and all the shirts in another. This will save searching through the suitcase to coordinate clothes.

• Buy each child a small duffel bag. Let them pack their own clothes (appropriate for the destination) and special toys—only what will fit in the bag. Duffel bags fit easily into a crowded car or under the seat of a plane, and are light and easy to carry. A child can also carry it without help. (6-10 yrs.)

• When traveling by car from Houston to Washington, a mother of an eight and a ten-year old gave each child a certain amount of money at the beginning of the trip. This was for buying souvenirs along the way or any other special purchase. Mom and Dad agreed to pay for food, lodging, and postcards only. This "allowance" was supplemented every other day with an additional $1.00. Both parents and children were happy with the way everything worked out. (7-10 yrs.)

• These same two children, David and Jenny, lost a nickle from their allowance each time any squabbling was heard from the back seat. (7-10 yrs.)

• If you notify our library in advance, the librarian will select books for you and put them together in a vacation pack.

IMPORTANT: Take along your pediatrician's phone number and your local toll-free Poison Control Center number.

Clean and Comfortable
• Keep a wet soapy washcloth in a plastic bag for fast cleanups, as well as a plain wet one in a separate bag.

• Or carry an empty squeeze bottle filled with water and soap.

• Eliminate spills in the car by using an old plastic baby bottle filled with fruit juice. Clip an opening in the tip of the nipple, invert it inside the bottle, and insert a straw through the hole. There's no chance of a spill, and the child feels very independent because he or she can manage the drink without help. (2-5 yrs.)

• Instead of taking pillows along for the children to use when they nap, take along pieces of foam. They'll fit under the seat when they're not in use.

• Hang a child's shoe bag over the window to block out the sun. You'll also have storage space in the "pockets" for some of your child's favorite toys.

• Stop at a playground for your travel break so your child can work off all that extra energy.

• Carry a little stale bread in your car; it's fun to feed the birds and squirrels at rest stops.

Games

• When you go on long trips, keep the children busy by play-ing games: counting cows or horses; finding as many different state license plates as possible; looking for different plants, buildings, and houses; or watching for things that begin with the same letter as the child's first name. (3-10 yrs.)

• Another game is "I spy." For example, "I see something that is blue." Have them ask questions that can be answered with a "yes" or "no" and limit the things "spied" to articles in the car. (3-10 yrs.)

• Make a short trip a mystery trip by having the children guess where they are going. (3-10 yrs.)

• Plan a scavenger hunt. Give your child a list of things to look for on the trip. (A picture list will do for one too young to read.) (3-10 yrs.)

• As you drive, have your child think of opposites. Examples: big car, small car; red light, green light; front of car, back of car. (3-7 yrs.)

• Matt, a nine-year-old we know, says computer games are his favorite travel toys.

• Play "Simon says" in the car. "Simon says smile," "Simon says wiggle your toes," etc. This keeps your children busy, and also lets them use up excess energy. (3-7 yrs.)

• Buy a supply of different card games before the trip begins. Hand these out each day as surprises. Your children will look forward to the next day of travel and will be kept occupied with their new "toy" during the trip. (8-10 yrs.)

• Some board games come with pieces that are held in grooved spaces. One of these is a traveling scrabble game. This is a great entertainer and an educational way to pass the time. The whole family can join in. (8-10 yrs.)

For more games

Kids' Book of Games for Cars, Trains, and Planes, by Rudi McToots. (New York: Bantam Books, Inc., 1980.)

Games for Children While Traveling, by Sid Hedges. (New York: Grosset and Dunlop, 1973.)

Activities

• Travel Toys:

1. Pencils and crayons
2. Paper
3. Magic Markers
4. Books
5. Unbreakable mirror
6. Whistle (if you can stand the noise)
7. Puppets
8. Crossword puzzles for different age levels
9. A kaleidoscope
10. Snap together blocks or beads
11. Binoculars
12. A flashlight to flicker around in the dark
13. Magnetic letters (Attach them to a metal cookie sheet/work table.)
14. Sketch pads
15. Computer games

• A box of pipe cleaners (colored ones are nicer) can be transformed into a menagerie, a family, or almost anything. These are great for car trips and when the journey is over, untangle them and you're ready to use them again. (3-8 yrs.)

• Cut pictures from magazines before you leave on a trip. Give your child paper and tape to create collages from the pictures you provide. (3-7 yrs.)

• Children can play tic-tac-toe or "connect the dots" on a chalkboard or a magic slate. You won't need to take along a lot of paper. (5-10 yrs.)

• Before leaving, have each child draw a picture and cut it into small pieces. Save as a puzzle to give to a traveling companion to assemble. (Never take along sharp objects like scissors in the car.) (4-10 yrs.)

• Give each child a grab bag that has been filled with odds and ends. After the children have touched and guessed all the contents, let them open the bags and enjoy the goodies. It may contain a pencil, an eraser, or even an apple. (3-8 yrs.)

• Play a scribble game. A friend draws a scribble on paper and the partner uses his imagination to interpret it. (4-10 yrs.)

• Have one child pretend he or she is looking into a mirror and have the other child pretend to be the mirror image. (4-10 yrs.)

• Take along your hose phone. Instructions in the "To Make for In or Out" section.

• Mark your route on a road map. Point to the cities you go through, the bridges you cross, and any other landmarks your child can identify on the map. (4-10 yrs.)

• Plan your trip with the children. They'll enjoy looking at a map to see where you are going, and will even help navigate along the way. (5-10 yrs.)

• Before long trips, we tape new records along with old favorites for our children to listen to in the car. (2-10 yrs.)

• There are also excellent cassettes that you can purchase called "Little Thinker Tapes," available through Discovery Toys. They contain forty-five minutes of a story about a particular subject, covering such topics as sports, outer space, and the circus, among others. They are informative, have music, and the children can participate by drawing pictures about what they hear on the tape. These tapes have made many of our long trips pleasant and quick-moving for the whole family. (4-8 yrs.)

• Another take-along tape is "Teach your Child Creative Expression," by Dr. Charles Patrick.

• Take along a blank tape, too. Let your children sing, recite, and tell stories. (4-10 yrs.)

• If you don't suffer from motion sickness, an enjoyable way to pass the time is by reading to your children. Arlene, mother of a school-age child, suggests reading either the *Hardy Boys Mysteries* or *Nancy Drew Mysteries* to your children. The chapters are short, easy to read, and always end on a note of suspense. (8-10 yrs.)

• She also suggests taking along a book called *Mad Libs*, published by Price, Stearn, and Sloane. Children fill in blanks with different parts of speech and form "silly" final sentences. These are fun and good grammar practice, too. (8-10 yrs.)

Taking Along Meals and Snacks
• Avoid salty foods when traveling. First, you'll be searching for cold drinks and then for restrooms.

• Air-tight containers are very handy for traveling. You can keep foods cool and dry by freezing water in one leakproof container and stacking it next to another container filled with food.

• Freeze ice in a small cup with a snap-on leakproof lid, and place it in a larger bowl. Put food around the cup; the food will stay cold but untouched by the melting ice. If your child gets thirsty, the melted ice in the cup provides a refreshing drink.

• I always place meal-size portions of baby's favorite cereal in a small plastic container and add the correct amount of powdered formula. When the baby is ready to eat, I just add water to the cereal along with my child's favorite fruit, and all is ready. This method is perfect for short trips, or if we're invited to a friend's for dinner. It's much more convenient than carrying along the entire box of cereal, and I'm assured that my child will have something he or she likes to eat.

• Carry snacks in an air-tight container. This way they won't crumble all over your purse or bag and will stay fresh.

• Use an empty coffee can or a large empty juice can for heating up bottles on the road. Place the bottle in the can and fill it with very hot water.

• A large thermos is handy, too. Any restaurant along the way will fill it with boiling water you can use to mix or heat formula, and to make tea, coffee, instant soups, or oatmeal

• If you're planning a picnic along the way, pack a picnic basket in reverse of unloading. (Tablecloth on top.)

• Wrap individual place settings of flatware in a napkin or two and secure with a colorful pipe cleaner.

• Save the individual packets of ketchup, mustard, sugar, salt, pepper, etc., that you receive with your meal at fast food places and restaurants. They may come in handy for picnics or for packing lunches for school-age children.

• Make a large number of sandwiches at once and freeze them. They will be thawed by lunch time.

• Cut sandwiches differently to identify the preferences of each child. Some will want mayonnaise and some mustard, (i.e. one is cut diagonally, one in squares, one in thirds, etc.)

• Put ice cubes in a large plastic bag in the cooler. When they melt, water won't be all over your food.

• Freeze the ice cubes for your cooler in 12-oz. juice cans. These giant ice cubes will last longer.

The Seashore
• For beach fun, don't forget:

Buckets	A thermos of juice
Shovels	Suntan oil
Ball or Frisbee	Comb or brush
Plastic containers for sand play	Camera
Adult-size shovel for digging a wading pool or "sand playpen"	Towels

• Take your infant seat to the beach with you. Rent an umbrella and your infant will be protected from the sun.

• If you're taking a playpen to the beach, place large jar lids under the legs to keep them from sinking into the sand. (This works well in a back yard, too.)

• When my daughter was at the crawling stage, our sunbathing was constantly interrupted. We spent most of the day chasing her down to the shoreline until my husband decided to dig a shallow hole in the sand and place her in her "sandbox playpen," with an umbrella overhead. She and her playmate, Alex, were quite happy, and we could relax. (Never leave your child unattended at the beach.)

To keep sand out of your picnic, eat indoors.

• To make a tote for your beach toys and other equipment, attach curtain rings around the outside of one of your larger beach towels. String a cord through the rings and tie the ends to make a drawstring. Place all your beach equipment on the towel, then pull the cord together on your tote/beach towel.

• To keep beach blankets flat, fill jugs with sand and put them on the corners of the blanket. If you don't want to be bothered carrying jugs, place some mounds of sand on the corners.

• Take a kite along to the beach because there is always a nice breeze. Your toddler will enjoy watching or helping you manuever the kite.

• For an older child, a frisbee is a lot of fun.

• Rubber-soled slippers are good for the beach when your child has to walk on hot sand.

• Plastic sandals or thongs also protect feet when the sun gets hot. Plastic sandals that buckle can be worn in the water to protect feet from stones or shells. Avoid thongs in the water, though, because they will slip off.

• Place a bucket of water outside the door to your beach house or motel room so everyone can dip their feet for an extra clean-up.

• Save food scraps to feed the seagulls.

• Put a meat tenderizer paste on a jellyfish sting to ease the pain.

Camping
• Don't forget the First Aid Kit and the First Aid Book.

• Before the real camping trip, a veteran camper advises having a pretend trip in your back yard. Set up the tent, have a cookout, even spend the night outdoors. Your child will love it. Then, pick some place nearby for your first attempt.

• Rent camping equipment, and try it out before buying. Many retail stores rent equipment on a daily basis. Check the "Yellow Pages" under "Rentals."

• If possible, camp in the late spring or early fall when camp grounds are less crowded.

• Don't overpack. Most camp grounds have their own laundromats. Purchase your diapers along the way.

• Camping grounds usually contain only showers for bathing. A friend suggests taking a plastic baby tub to serve as a suitcase along the way and tub by night.

• Instead of trying to have a real campfire, take along a grill or hibachi and some charcoal. This will be much easier to manage than a campfire, and your children will be just as happy with this method.

• Store matches in an air-tight tin so they'll stay dry.

• Consult *The Boy Scouts' Handbook* for excellent camping tips.

53 *more* helpful hints on:

About Town
And All Around

• Never go anywhere if your child is not rested. Even if you only plan to pick up a few things at the grocery store, you would be wise to wait and let your child take a nap. It is easier to deal with a crowd than to deal with a cranky child.

• Don't tell a child about an outing until a few minutes before you leave. Plans always can fall through, and a little one has trouble accepting disappointment.

• Always keep a checklist of the things you may need when you go out somewhere with your baby. Record information on a 3 x 5 card and keep it handy, revised, and ready if you need it in a hurry.

• Sample diaper bag checklist:

Bottle or can of juice	A small roll of tape to repair the tabs on a disposable diaper, or extra pins for your cloth diaper
Non-perishable snacks	
Bib	
Spare pacifier	Powder
Diapers, of course	Lap pad or sheet of plastic
Baby wipes or cotton balls dipped in oil	Change of clothing
	Lightweight jacket or sweater
Plastic bag to discard disposable diapers or to hold dirty diapers until you get home	Book
	Small toys
	A favorite blanket

• On a pleasant weekend day, pack a picnic lunch right after breakfast, and it will be ready to eat wherever you are. Take it along on a shopping trip and find a picnic spot, or just spread it out in the backyard at lunch time.

• Carriages are great for tiny ones, but once your baby decides to sit up a little, the view is restricted. Place an infant seat in the carriage so your baby can sit almost upright and look around. Caution: Make sure it doesn't go too high above the carriage.

• To avoid bickering on outings when you have an uneven number of children, let one of them invite a friend to come along. Even numbers seem to get into less trouble. (3-10 yrs.)

Places to Go
• Go to the zoo at feeding time. You'll learn what the animals eat, and also your children will get to see how they eat. (3-10 yrs.)

• In the winter when it's too cold to go to the zoo, visit a pet store instead. (2-10 yrs.)

• On a rainy day I give my child a dollar and we go to a five and dime store. He enjoys his shopping spree. (4-8 yrs.)

• When we want to get out but have nowhere to go, we take a round-trip ride on a bus or subway. (2-10 yrs.)

• Plan a field trip to your spouse's office or just meet your spouse for lunch. (3-10 yrs.)

• Arrange for your child to visit the work areas of favorite spots such as a fast food restaurant, a bakery, a doughnut shop, or an ice cream shop. He or she will enjoy seeing how the food is prepared. It's also fun to visit backstage at a play, puppet show, or a circus, if it can be arranged. (3-10 yrs.)

Other favorite spots are: a farm, a hardware store, the library, an aquarium, a greenhouse, a police station, a firehouse, a brewery, a farmer's market, a fish or chicken hatchery, and a toy store. (3-10 yrs.)

• Take your child to an outdoor concert in the summer. Pack a picnic lunch and enjoy your day. You'll not have to worry about disturbing anyone in the audience. (2-10 yrs.)

In A Crowd
• If it's going to be crowded, take along your back pack instead of the stroller. Strollers get in the way in crowds.

• Buy some self-adhesive labels and put your child's name on one of them. Stick the label to the back of your child's shirt so it cannot be removed.

• Give your child a whistle to blow if he or she needs you.

• Make an arrangement with your older children to meet at an agreed upon location in case anyone becomes separated.

The Grocery Store

• Take your newborn's infant seat inside. Rather than crowding your child, the seat, and your groceries into one cart, use two. Push the cart with your baby in front of you so your child is facing you and can see that you are nearby. Smile and talk to him or her while you shop, and pull the second cart and groceries behind you. (This works better in a store with wide aisles!)

• When your baby starts to sit up, take a man's necktie with you to tie the baby into the grocery cart. (6 mo.-9 mo.)

• Tie a small toy or rattle or teether to your child's shirt. It's something to keep the little one busy while you shop, and you won't have to worry about losing it. Don't make the string too long. (6 mo.-2 yrs.)

• Do everything in your power to keep your child in the cart and away from the grocery store displays. Give your child a piece of fruit to hold onto and tell him or her to take good care of it. Make your child a cereal necklace to wear and munch on. Take a book to look at or a toy your child has not played with recently. (18 mo.-3 yrs.)

• To keep your child from demanding cookies and candies as you shop, stop at the fruit counter first and give him or her an apple to eat. An apple is nutritious and takes a long time to chew. (2-4 yrs.)

Or have your child select *one* nutritious snack and have him or her hold onto it while you shop. This will keep your child occupied and in the cart. Or spend the trip choosing one sugarless treat. (3-6 yrs.)

• Ask the grocer for a shallow box and put your jars of baby food inside or take a box lid along. This will save you from having to lift every jar out individually at the checkout counter.

• If you must shop before your errands, take along a cooler to keep frozen foods from spoiling.

• Your older child can help with the shopping. If you only need one or two things, have him or her shop for them; your child can carry the list, push the cart, make the selection, and pay for the purchase. (This is also a good time to give lessons on nutrition and good eating habits.) (6-10 yrs.)

• If you're having guests for dinner, have your older child plan the menu and go along to make the food purchases. You could also involve him or her in the cooking and clean-up. (6-10 yrs.)

More tips in:
The Supermarket, by Ann and Harlow Rockwell. (New York: Macmillan Publishing Co., Inc., 1979.) (2-5 yrs.)

Eating Out
• Feed the baby before you go to the restaurant, or at least have some small snack to keep him or her occupied while you wait to be served.

Save fancy restaurants for evenings when you have a sitter.

• When you take your child's entire meal to the resturant, wrap each item in a different kind of paper. The child will enjoy opening his "presents." Use aluminum foil, plastic wrap, or even wrapping paper for a piece of fruit. (2-7 yrs.)

• Choose a cafeteria-style restaurant. Service is faster.

• Go to a restaurant *before* your children are really hungry, or give them a snack to make them more patient while you wait to be served.

• Some dentist's clips or sweater clips attached to a napkin or paper towel are a good substitute for a forgotten bib.

• When juice is the beverage your child prefers, carry along several cans of juice, (the small one-serving size). It's not a bad idea to have extra cans of juice in your car or purse all the time. Children get thirsty in the most inconvenient places!

• In preparation for eating out, conduct conversations at the dinner table in restaurant voices. (This is also good practice for church, movies, and other places where children should lower their voices.)

The Movies

• It really gets dark in a theater. This is something you're used to, but it can be frightening to your child. Explain about the darkness before you go, and assure him or her that you'll be very close by. For practice, make some popcorn, have some snacks on hand, and enjoy a television show together in the dark.

• Bring your child's infant seat or booster seat with you to the movies. Your child will be more comfortable and will have no trouble seeing over anyone's head.

• Save some money and avoid a crowd by going to a matinee. Some theaters have twilight shows where admission is $1.50 while other places have one afternoon show per week when you can see a movie for only $1.00.

• Popcorn and the movies go together. Take along some empty milk cartons or bags of popcorn with you to the drive-in.

• Can't get a sitter? Take the kids to the movies with you—the drive-in that is. Put on their pajamas, pack some sleep equipment (pillows, car bed, etc.) and they'll be asleep before you know it. Enjoy your night out.

Museums

• A magnifying glass or binoculars are great for taking a closer look at fossils, insects, or artwork and will keep your child busy and interested longer.

• Make the gift shop your first stop at any museum. Help your children select postcards and use them for a "scavenger hunt" while you browse. Your kids will have fun finding the things pictured on the postcards which will serve as a reminder of their visit.

• Carry your child in a backpack instead of a stroller. He or she will be able to see everything better when perched up high and you won't be bumping into anyone with the stroller.

• Some museums rent headsets for a small fee. This way, your child will receive information while being fascinated by the voice heard at each display.

• Don't miss the free movies some museums offer.

Just Visiting

• Enjoy your visit. Don't spend your time following your child around making sure he or she doesn't touch fragile or dangerous objects. Take along some favorite toys or a box of toys not played with for some time. This will keep your child occupied and out of trouble—at least for a little while. (1-5 yrs.)

• Have a prearranged "settle down" signal with your older child such as your finger touching or tapping your knee. When he or she sees this sign, your child knows it means settle down. Your secret gets the message across without embarrassment. (5-10 yrs.)

• When you visit relatives who do not have children around, carry a bag of large rubber bands and loop these around the knobs of cabinets to lock the cupboards and keep your children from harm.

• If you're unsure of your host's menu, take along a favorite food and drink so your fussy eater will have something he or she likes.

• When there's no high chair available, improvise. Strap your child to a chair with a man's belt.

• No room in the car for a portable crib, playpen, or a high chair? Consider renting this very necessary equipment when you reach your destination. Check in the "Yellow Pages" under "Rentals."

• For an older child, a sleeping bag is a convenient take-along-bed. Whenever we visit and there's a shortage of sleeping spaces, my son is always eager to be on the floor in his sleeping bag.

48 *more* helpful hints on:

Help With
The Housework

Housework Timesavers
• Set the table for breakfast before you go to bed. This will be one less thing to do in the morning.

• You child's naptime is *not* your cleaning time; it's your time to relax. Dust and scrub along with your child. He or she will feel grown up and you will get some work done. If you have an infant, wheel the bassinet around from room to room and talk or sing to your little one while you work.

• While you're ironing, talk with your children. Tell stories, sing, let them have their own iron and ironing board. They will enjoy this time with you, and you won't feel that you have to do work only when they're asleep. (2-10 yrs.)

• When any type of fruit juice gets accidentally spilled on the kitchen floor, it seems to remain a sticky mess even after wiping up. Rather than getting out the mop and bucket, I have a spray bottle handy containing a mixture of 1/4 part vinegar to 3/4 parts water. After wiping up most of the spill, squirt this mixture on the area and wipe. The vinegar/water mixture will remove the stickiness.

• My friend Barbara's son enjoyed being held, and being close to his mother, as most babies do. Whenever she had housework that *had* to be done, she placed him in his front carrier. Mother and son were close, and her hands were free. (NB)

• If you're constantly running to the refrigerator to fill a cup of juice for your child, save yourself some work. Leave a cup of juice already poured in the refrigerator and let your children help themselves. (3-5 yrs.)

• Or have a thermos in your refrigerator. They now make jugs that have a push button for the juice. This saves on spills. (3-10 yrs.)

• Keep a wide putty knife handy in the kitchen. It is good for scraping up mashed foods, squashed crayons and clay, and that spilled cereal that turns to cement when it hits the floor.

• Save on dishwashing. Use paper plates and cups.

• When you make your child's bed, put the top sheet on lengthwise across the width of the bed. It doesn't matter if the top sheet doesn't reach the bottom of the bed because your child's feet won't reach that far anyway. Do the same for the blanket. This will keep your child from getting uncovered at night and help keep him or her from falling out of bed. Best of all, making the bed in the morning is much easier.

• A very tidy friend uses cafe curtain hooks to pinch two corners of the towel together over the towel rack. This keeps her child from pulling the towel off every time he dries his hands.

• Attach a roll of paper towels to the side of the bathroom vanity. This way you'll wash fewer towels.

• Designate a section of your bookshelf specifically for library books and make sure your children return all such books to this shelf. This saves time searching for the library books that might become mixed up with your own.

An Ounce of Prevention
• Cut a sponge to fit your soap dish. When you put the soap on the sponge, there'll be no gooey mess.

• To keep bathroom tiles shiny, coat them with furniture polish. It minimizes soapy build-up.

• Prevent greasy fingermarks in your stairways by painting them with rough-textured paint. This will discourage little hands from sliding along the wall on the way up or down.

• Attach a curtain rod half way down on your screen door to keep the screen from being pushed out.

• Cars, trucks, and other push toys have a way of crashing into furniture. To protect against nicks and scratches, place a piece of sponge or foam rubber on the edge of the toys.

• The same goes for your child's walker. A little piece of foam rubber will protect your furniture from scratches while he or she zips around the house.

• When you use a cool mist humidifier, not only does it put moisture in the air, but it also makes the area around the humidifier really wet. To protect your floor or carpeting, place a rubber sheet or a piece of plastic under the humidifier before you plug it in.

Working Together
• For housework help, consider hiring a high school student. You won't have to pay much, and he or she may turn out to be someone you could use for babysitting. If the student comes to your house often enough to help out, your child will come to know him or her and to accept his or her presence more easily than a new babysitter.

• Grandma's most successful clean-up strategies are: (1) Set the timer and see how many things you and your child can pick up before it rings. (2) Make a chore grab bag. Fill it with things that have to be done and let each child reach in and grab a job. It's much more fun and chores are more readily accepted. (3) At the end of the day, everyone can agree to pick up six items and put them away. (4) With older children, leave notes around requesting that a job be done. For example, on the door to your child's room you may write, "Please clean me."

• Outdoor clean-up is easy too if you paint or mark with chalk the spaces where you want the riding toys to be parked.

• Using the toy storage hints in the "Toys" section, you'll find playroom cleaning easier and so will your child. Let your children and their friends put the toys in the proper containers after each play session. The playroom will never be too messy to play in, and the toys will be in place.

• Fill a squeeze bottle with cleaning solution and let your child help wash windows. Don't use a spray bottle; your child can point it the wrong way and squirt cleaning fluid into the eyes. The same goes for aerosol cleaners. (3-10 yrs.)

• Children also love to help scrub. Give them a mop and bucket and let them practice on the back porch or patio before you let them loose in the kitchen. (3-10 yrs.)

• Dusting, cleaning, and "emptying out" can be fun. Who knows what surprises they'll find? I let them help and get all those "mañana" jobs done. Cleaning out closets, kitchen cabinets, the refrigerator, and bureau drawers can be especially fun for your children. (3-10 yrs.)

Wash Day
• Sometimes the hardest part of doing the laundry is getting it to the laundry room. Take the wash downstairs and sort it in the evening. Place the first load in the washer and then the next morning it will only take you a minute to put the soap in the machine and start it.

• Instead of combining everyone's laundry for one big wash day, make sure each child has his or her own hamper. When it's full enough for one load, wash it all in cold water so the colors won't run. (no sorting involved) Since it all goes into the same room, folding and putting away is easy, too.

• Save time sorting laundry. Have your family tie any clothing that needs extra care in a big knot (i.e. with a missing button or a hole).

You'll be able to pick the clothing out easily and will save a lot of time usually spent checking and sorting.

• That outgrown bassinet makes an excellent laundry basket on wheels. If you're carting wet things, line it with a piece of plastic to protect the wood.

• Playing in sand and dirt is lots of fun. Pockets and cuffs are great places for all that dirt to hide. Use the attachment on your vacuum cleaner to remove all the dirt before you put the clothing into the wash.

• If you can never get that favorite blanket away from your child for washing, tear it in half. Keep one half where it can always be found to replace the one you want to take back from your little one. Chances are, your child will never suspect the switch.

Stains and Cleanup
• Tape a stain removal chart on your washing machine. Refer to the chart and treat the stain as soon as possible. Overnight soaking helps get out difficult stains.

Here are some stain removal instructions for those of us with little ones around:

• *Ballpoint Pen:* From walls and woodwork: Dampen a cloth with distilled white vinegar and blot with an absorbent cloth. Repeat as often as necessary.

From fabric: Apply lukewarm glycerin, then blot the stain with an absorbent cloth. Keep the stain moist with glycerin and repeat as many times as necessary. Flush with water and apply chlorine bleach to the wash if any traces remain.

• *Blood Stains:* Treat immediately by soaking or rubbing in cold water until the stain almost disappears, then wash. If the stain remains, apply a few drops of ammonia, and wash again.

If the stain is already set, make a cornstarch and cold water paste and spread thickly over the stain. Let it dry and brush it off. You may have to repeat this application.

• *Chewing Gum:* From hair: Rub in cold cream or baby oil. Use a dry rag and pull down on the strands of hair to remove the gum.

From furniture or rugs: Place an ice cube on it until it is frozen and it will crack off.

From clothing: Put the item in a bag in the freezer. The gum will freeze and then you can chip it off.

• *Crayon:* From painted walls and woodwork: Sprinkle dry baking soda onto a damp cloth and rub gently. Liquid detergent or silver polish applied directly to the mark should also work.

From clothing: Dampen the stain and rub in undiluted liquid detergent until it forms thick suds. Work this in well, then rinse. Repeat if necessary.

• *Egg Stains:* Sponge the spot with cold water or soak the whole article of clothing in cold water, then launder as usual. Caution: Never use hot water on an egg stain. It will set.

• *Fingerprints:* Mix 1/2 cup ammonia and 1/2 cup washing soda in a gallon of warm water. Dip a cloth into the solution and rub gently.

• *Food Coloring:* From clothing: Rub with toothpaste, let dry, and rinse in cold water.

• *Fruit Juice:* Treat stain promptly with *cold* water to keep it from setting, then soak for 30 minutes in a solution of 1 quart warm water, 1/2 teaspoon liquid hand dishwashing detergent, and 1 T ammonia. Rinse with water and wash.

Toothpaste

• *G r a s s Stains:* Sponge with alcohol. Test the material for color-fastness before trying this. Or, you may work liquid detergent or shampoo into the stain and rinse. Launder as usual.

• *Paint:* Remove housepaint from your child's skin with margarine or cooking oil.

• *Pencil Marks:* Remove from wallpaper by erasing them with stale bread.

• *Tempera Paint:* From walls: Rub gently with dry baking soda on a dampened cloth.

• *Urine Stains:* Soak the item for 30 minutes in a solution of 1 quart warm water, 1/2 teaspoon liquid hand dishwashing detergent, and 1 T ammonia. Rinse with clear water and wash.

From bathroom floor tiles: Apply liquid vegetable oil to the spot and let it set for a minute or so before wiping. You may have to repeat the application.

From rugs and furniture: Use club soda or white vinegar.

• **WARNING: Keep all cleaning supplies out of children's reach.**

Kids love to polish brass-pour polish into a lid, give her rags, cotton balls and swabs.

Lid screwed on!

news-paper→

41 *more* helpful hints on:

Great Escapes

Babysitters

• Call your local high school and talk with the guidance counselors. They will be able to recommend dependable students who babysit.

• If your sitter is a high school student, he or she will be busy with school activities in addition to sitting for others. Set up a date on a weekly basis so you'll be sure of your sitter's availability.

• Talk to neighbors whose opinions you respect for names of babysitters they use. Some of your neighbors may have teen-age or college-age children. You may also have elderly neighbors who enjoy children and who could use the extra money.

• Some senior citizens groups do babysitting. Some churches also offer babysitting services at reasonable rates. They call this service "Mother's Morning Out."

• Often, you may find that single friends or friends without children (men or women) would enjoy babysitting your children.

• Before you leave your children with a new babysitter, let them get acquainted. Invite the sitter over for lunch and a visit. If you cannot arrange a convenient time have the sitter come over before you have to leave. The children will feel more comfortable getting to know their sitter while you are still there.

• Leave an article of clothing with the sitter that is familiar to your baby. Many times if the sitter wears the article of clothing, (a bathrobe, for example) the baby stops crying.

• Let your children look forward to having a babysitter. Plan something special just for the children to do with the sitter, or start a game or craft and have them complete it when the sitter arrives.

• Hire a babysitter to watch your children and put them to bed for you when you are having company over.

• As children begin to feel that babysitters are an insult to their emerging maturity, be sure the babysitter is a number of years older than the child. Try to choose one who is like a big sister or brother and whom the child admires. (8-10 yrs.)

• Call babysitters, "Mother's Helper." It's less insulting to an older child. (8-10 yrs.)

• Give older children responsibility for the younger ones. (6-10 yrs.)

• If you are taking your child *to* the babysitter, include a permission slip for treatment, along with a name and number where you or your spouse can be reached. Tape this permanently to the inside of the diaper bag and point out its location to the sitter.

• To clarify your rules when dealing with sitters, make a few photocopies of a brief contract. It can contain such things as no phone calls, no visitors, hourly rate, and what food is available for the sitter. Both you and your sitter can sign it.

• Point out the location of the First Aid Kit, your emergency phone list (sample follows), and your sitter sheet (sample follows) in addition to the location of the phones, the television, and the fire extinguisher. Also show your sitter where the hospital release slip is located (sample follows) in case you cannot be reached.

• Cover your sitter sheet with clear plastic adhesive so you can make any changes with a grease pencil re: bedtime, food, etc., whenever you go out.

- *Sitter Sheet:*
(Special Information For the Sitter)

Where parents can be reached: _____

When parents will return: _____

Names and nicknames of children: _____

Number of neighbor(s) who can help: _____

T.V. rules for children: _____

Sleeping arrangements: _____

Location of cothing, toys, diapers, and other special equipment

_____

_____

_____

Bedtime: _____

Meal (or snack) time: _____

Favorite stories or activities: _____

Where children play: _____

Dangerous or "off limits" areas in the house:_____

Sitter Privileges: _____

IMPORTANT: Specific directions to your house. (So sitter can direct others to your home in case of emergency.)

_____

_____

_____

_____

Sample Hospital Release Form:

I (we)_____the legal guardian(s) of_____ ,

a minor, authorize_____to consent to x-ray, examination,

anesthesia, medical or surgical diagnosis, or treatment and hospital

care to the minor under the supervision of a physician or surgeon

when the need for such treatment is immediate and efforts to contact

me (us) are unsuccessful.

Signed _____ Date _____

Child's Doctor_____

Child's allergies _____

Medicines child is taking _____

• **Don't be frightened into cancelling your plans by a child who screams when you leave;** the screaming will probably stop in a few minutes. And remember that the only way your child will learn to trust you is to see you leave and return.

For further information
Pocket Guide to Babysitting. This pamphlet is available through the Government Printing Office. Write for the current price to:

> Superintendent of Documents
> U.S. Government Printing Office
> Washington, D.C. 20402
> Publication No. 017-091-00197-9

Co-ops
• If you know several parents in your neighborhood who have children the same age as your child, you may be interested in forming a babysitting co-op. Instead of paying for the service, choose a secretary who can keep track of the number of hours each member uses the service. For example, if member No. 1 leaves his or her child with member No. 2 for two hours, member No. 1 is minus two hours and member No. 2 is credited with two hours.

• To make it fair to all, rotate the secretary position each month, and allot the secretary some free hours credit for recording everyone's credits and debits. Allow time-and-a-half credit for babysitting more than one child, and double time for the weekend sitter.

• Let your child get to know the people who'll be sitting with him or her. If it's summer time, organize a picnic at the park where parents and children can meet to talk and play. Notice which children your child favors, and invite parents and children over for a visit. You will both feel more comfortable when it's time to take advantage of the co-op.

• In addition to providing each co-op member with a list of the members and their phone numbers, include the names and ages of each member's children. It would be helpful to leave your child with children of his or her own age.

• Start a co-operative playgroup for your toddler. The group can be formed when the children are under a year old, and the parents can get to know one another while the babies become familiar with the new surroundings. When they have adjusted to the routine, a couple of the parents can plan to leave each week and get in a little time of their own. Four to five children seem to be a good number, and can alternate meeting at one another's homes. Each parent should have a list containing each child's doctor's phone number, other emergency numbers, and a hospital release form in case a child must be taken to an emergency room. See sample in "Babysitters" section.

A Little Freedom and Freebies, Too

• Take off for the weekend! Leave your children overnight with a sitter you can trust. Even if you only go five miles away, you will get a needed break.

• Hire a babysitter to come over and supervise your children so you or your spouse can get "away." You don't even have to leave the house. Get a good book and go to your room. Put on a set of headsets so you won't hear any of the commotion, and listen to your favorite music.

If it feels good to scream — the freezer muffles the sound

• Set your alarm to go off one half-hour early. Keep a book or magazine near your bed and enjoy your time alone.

• When it's all really too much for you, HIDE. Let your spouse know you'll be "out" for a while, then find a secret spot (even the attic) and crouch! Listen to the chaos and feel like a private little kid. It does wonders to restore your calm.

• Hire a teenager to work as a "parents' helper" after school.

• Shut yourself in the bathroom with something to read.

• Get out of the house a little. Take a class at the local community college—something that has always interested you—learn a craft, a language, take yoga, or do aerobic dancing.

• Spend an evening in the magazine section of the library.

• Join a diet group if you need it!

• Many childbirth preparation classes offer parent groups for new Moms and Dads. Volunteers speak to new parents on subjects of interest to them such as: how to make your own baby food, tips on child safety, instructions for learning to sew clothing for your children. There is no charge to attend the meeting, and it's a wonderful way to meet parents with children the same age as your own. If there is nothing like this where you live, form one. You'll be surprised by how many "parent specialists" you'll find to speak.

• Get together regularly with new parents and just talk. It's reassuring to know everyone is having the same problems you are!

• Form a book club, a craft club, a cooking club, etc., with friends and neighbors. This is a good way to get out of the house on a regular basis, talk with others, and *it's free!*

• Find a senior citizen in your neighborhood and offer to do grocery shopping, mow the lawn, etc., in exchange for babysitting.

• Your local library offers free programs for pre-schoolers and elementary-school age children. These may include puppet shows, movies, or story times. Call in advance. Some libraries require you to sign up to attend.

• After school is out most churches have church camps. These usually last for two weeks, are open for pre-schoolers and elementary-school age children, and they're FREE. Why not send your child to several during the summer? It is not necessary to be a member of the church to attend.

• Consider summer camp. You don't have to ship your child away to take advantage of this. Some "summer camps" meet daily at the local playground and have organized crafts and activities.

• Children and parents can form their own neighborhood summer camp. There are always talented parents around who may offer their skills for free or for a small fee. Arrange a special time for everyone to meet and your children will enjoy crafts, music, or any other talent a parent can contribute. If enough parents aren't available, many teachers are free during the summer and may be willing to help out.

For free offers for children

Freebies for Kids, by Jeffrey Feinman. (New York: Wanderer Books, 1979.) (7-10 yrs.)

Or, *Whole Kids' Catalog and Second Whole Kids' Catalog,* by Peter Cardozo. (New York: Bantam Books, Inc., 1975.) (7-10 yrs.)

Books, Books, Books!

Books to Read Along With Children

The children's librarian at your local public library or school will have a suggested reading list for each age. Ask her for it and then help your children find the books on the list appropriate for them. This list was compiled by the Montgomery County Public Libraries, Montgomery County, Maryland for "The Early Years."

Sturdy Books for the Very Youngest
Where's Spot?, Hill

Family, Working, and others, Oxenbury.

Max's First Word, and others, Wells.

Lullabies and Sleepy Stories
Goodnight Moon, Brown.
Where Do Bears Sleep?, Hazen
Hush Little Baby, (Aliki).
Good Night Owl!, Hutchins.
Close Your Eyes, Marzollo.
What's In The Dark, Memling.
Goodnight, Goodnight, Rice.
On Mother's Lap, Scott.
A Good Day, A Good Night, Wheeler.
Lullabies and Night Songs, Wilder. J784.624
Bears Are Sleeping, Yulya. J784

Nursery Rhymes and Mother Goose
Johnny Crow's Garden, and *Fiddle-I-Fee*, Brooke.
All The Pretty Horses, Jeffers.
Over in the Meadow, Langstaff.
Mother Goose. (various editions; Wildsmith, Briggs, Provensen,, Rojankovsky, Tudor, Wright, Marshall.)
Ring O' Roses, Mother Goose. (L. Brooke, illus.)
Catch Me and Kiss Me and Say it Again, Watson.

Pictures to Talk About
Each Peach, Pear, Plum, Ahlberg.
Do You Want To Be My Friend?, Carle.
Where Is It?, Demi.
Turn About, Think About, Look About Book, Gardner.
Look!, Gay.
Take Another Look, Hoban.
Changes Changes, Hutchins.
Find the Cat, Livermore.
Magic Balloon, Mari.
Things To See, Matthiesen.
A Boy, A Dog, and A Frog, Meyer.
I Spy, Ogle.
Odd One Out, Peppe.
Noah's Ark, Spier.
Puzzles, Wildsmith.
But Where Is The Green Parrot?, Zacharias.

Beginning Picture Story Books

Three Billy Goats Gruff, Asbjornsen.
Sand Cake, Asch.
Buzz, Buzz, Buzz, Barton.
Green Eyes, Birnbaum.
Mr. Gumpys Outing, and others, Burningham.
Pancakes, Pancakes and *Very Hungry Caterpillar,* Carle.
Play With Me, Ets.
Angus and The Ducks and *Ask Mr. Bear,* Flack.
Corduroy, Freeman.
Mushroom In The Rain and *Ookie-Spooky,* Ginsburg.
Where's Spot?, Hill.
Rosie's Walk and *Titch,* Hutchins.
The Snowy Day, Keats.
Bundle Book, Krauss.
My Teddy Bear and *My Day on the Farm,* Nakatani.
The Box with Red Wheels and *Circus Baby,* Petersham.
New Blue Shoes and *Sam Who Never Forgets,* Rice.
Tell Me A Mitzi, Segal.
Where The Wild Things Are, Sendak.

Ourselves and Others
Black is Brown is Tan, Adoff.
I Feel, Ancona. J152.4
Shawn Goes To School, and others, Breinburg.
Faces and *Bodies,* Brenner. J612

Some of the Days of Everett Anderson, Clifton.
Will I Have A Friend? and *No Good In Art, and others*, Cohen.
Feelings, Dunn. J152.4
Just Me, Ets.
Willaby and *My Ballet Class*, Isadora.
Sara And The Door, Jensen.
How We Are Born and *How We Grow* also *How Our Bodies Work*, Kaufman. J612
Peter's Chair and *Whistle For Willie*, Keats.
My Doctor, My Nursery School, My Barber, I Like the Library, and others, Rockwell. J616
Sam, Scott.
Michael and *We Were Tired of Living in a House*, Skorpen.
Let's Be Enemies, Udry.
Alexander and the Terrible, Horrible, No Good, Very Bad Day, Viorst.
Noisy Nora, Wells.

Learning Concepts

Anno's Alphabet Book and *Anno's Counting Book*, Anno.
A B C, Burningham.
We Read: A to Z, Crews.
Two Lonely Ducks, Duvoisin.
Dancing in the Moon, Eichenberg.
A B C, Falls.
Jambo Means Hello and *Moja Means One*, Feelings.
ABC Bunny, Gag.
Count and See and *Push-Pull, Empty-Full*, Hoban.
The Rain Puddle, Holl.
My Feet Do and *My Hand Can*, Holzenthaler.
What's That?, Jensen
The Chicken and The Egg, Mari.
Where Is My Friend?, Maestro.
A B See, Ogle. J372.4145
Shapes, Reiss.
This Can Lick a Lollipop, Rothman.
Apples to Zippers, Ruben.
Best Word Book Ever, Scarry.
It Looked Like Split Milk, Shaw.

The Natural World

My Puppy Is Born, Cole. J636.7
Charlie Needs A Cloak, De Paola.
Gilberto and The Wind, Ets.
Ants Go Marching, Freschet.
Down To The Beach, Garelick.
The Wind Blew, Hutchins.

From Seed to Jack-O-Lantern, Johnson. J635.62
The Happy Day and *Carrot Seed,* Krauss.
Time Of Wonder, McCloskey.
Books For The Young Explorers, National Geographic Society.
        Spiders, Bason. J595.5
        Pandas, Grosvenor. J599.74443
Dinosaur Time, Parish. J568.1
Animals At Maple Hill Farm, Provensen.
Animals In The Zoo and *Animals On the Farm,* Rojankovsky.
Is This A Baby Dinosaur, Selsam. J500.1
Gobble, Growl, Grunt, Spier.
The Birth of Sunset's Kittens, Stevens. J636.8
When The Tide Goes Out, Waddell. J591.92
Look At A Calf, Wright. J637
Two Little Bears, Ylla.

Wheels and Work

Tony's Hard Work Day, Arkin.
Wheels and *Building A House,* Barton.
Mike Mulligan and His Steam Shovel, Burton
Freight Train and *Truck,* Crews.
The Boats On The River, Flack.
Dig, Drill, Dump, Fill, Hoban.
Best Train Set Ever, Hutchins.
Bear's Bicycle, McLeod.
Train, McPhail.
Machines, J621. and *Thruway* also *Toolbox,* Rockwell.
Crash! Bang! Boo!, Spier.
The Truck Book, Wolfe. J629.224

More Stories for Steady Listeners

Little Tim series, Ardizzone.
Madeline, Bemelmans.
Jim and The Beanstalk, Briggs.
Golden Goose Book, Brooke.
Babar series, Brunhoff.
The Boy Who Didn't Believe In Spring, Clifton.
Strega Nona, and others, De Paola.
In The Forest, Ets.
Story About Ping, Flack.
Millions of Cats and *Snippy and Snappy,* Gag.
Frog And Toad series, Lobel.
Blueberries For Sal and *Make Way For Ducklings,* McCloskey.
Tale of Peter Rabbit, Potter.

Curious George, Rey.
Three Bears and Fifteen Other Stories, Rockwell. J398.2
Tell Me A Mitzi, Segal.
Outside, Over There, Sendak.
Sylvester and The Magic Pebble, and others, Steig.
Three Little Pigs, (Blegvad, illus.)
Great Big Enormous Turnip, Tolstoy.
The Mitten, Tresselt.
What Mary Jo Wanted, and others, Udry.
Ira Sleeps Over, Waber.
Umbrella, Yashima.

About Birthdays

Secret Birthday Message, Carle.
Don't You Remember?, Clifton.
Pooh Party Book, Ellison. J793.2
Betty Crocker's Parties For Children, Freeman. J793.2
Happy Birthday, Sam, Hutchins.
Letter To Amy, Keats.
Me Day, Lexau.
Birthday Party Book, Ross. J793.2
Mr. Rabbit and The Lovely Present, Zolotow.

Fun and Nonsense

The Giant Jam Sandwich, Burroway.
May I Bring A Friend?, DeRegniers.
Don't Forget The Bacon, Hutchins.
George and Martha, Marshall.
Piggy In The Puddle, Pomerantz.
The Wedding Procession of The Rag Doll and The Broom Handle, Sandburg.
Rain Makes Applesauce, Scheer.
Chicken Soap With Rice and *Pierre,* Sendak.
Horton Hatches The Egg and *If I Ran The Zoo,* Seuss.
Crictor, Ungerer.

First Books for Early Readers

Where is Everybody?, Charlip.
This Is The House Where Jack Lives, Heilbroner.
Come And Have Fun, Hurd.
Wacky Wednesday, LeSieg.
Cat and Dog, Minarik.
Kitten Book and *Mouse Book,* Piers.
Cat In The Hat and *Hop On Pop,* Seuss.
Come To The Farm and *Come To The Zoo,* Tensen.

Special Feelings of Children

Abby and *Daddy*, Caines.
Amifika, Clifton.
New Girl At School, Delton.
Send Wendell, Gray.
She Come Bringing Me That Little Baby Girl, Greenfield.
I'm Moving, Hickman.
Whistle For Willie, Keats.
I Want Mama, Sharmat.
Moving Day, Tobias.
Tenth Good Thing About Barney, Viorst.
Are You Sad, Mama?, Winthrop.
Special Trade, Wittman.
Umbrella, Yashima.

Poetry

Honey, I Love, and Other Love Poems, Greenfield. J811
In The Middle Of The Trees, Kuskin. J811
Every Time I Climb A Tree, McCord. J811
Away We Go—100 Poems For The Very Young, McEwen. J808.81
Tamarindo Puppy, Pomerantz. J811

Songs and Games

Sally Go Round The Sun, Fowke. J398.8
Do Your Ears Hang Low, Glazer. J784.6
   Eye Winker, Tom Tinker, Chin Chopper. J796.13
Baby's Song Book, Poston. J784
Fireside Book of Children's Songs, Winn. J784.624
   What Shall We Do And Allee Galloo. J784.6

Sources For Parents And Children

This bibliography was compiled by Montgomery County Public Libraries, Children's Services, Montgomery County, Maryland.

About Children and Parents *(to age 5)*

Your Two Year Old—Terrible or Tender, Ames, Louise. (New York: Delacorte Press, 1974.)

Toddlers and Parents, Brazelton, T.B. (New York: Delacorte Press, 1974.)

Something's Wrong With My Child, Brutten, Milton. (New York: Harcourt Brace Jovanovich, Inc., 1973.)

Your Child Is A Person, Chess, Stella. (New York: Penguin Books, Inc., 1977.)

Black Child Care, Comer, James P. (New York: Simon & Schuster, Inc., 1975.)

How To Parent, Dodson, Fitzhugh. (New York: Nash Pub. Co., 1970.)

The Magic Years, Fraiberg, Selma H. (New York: Charles Scribner & Sons, 1959.)

Between Parent and Child, Ginott, Haim G. (New York: Macmillan Pub. Co., Inc., 1967.)

Right From The Start, A Guide To Non-Sexist Child Rearing, Greenburg, Selma. (Boston: Houghton Mifflin Co., 1978.)

The Father Book; Pregnancy and Beyond, Grad, Rae, R.N., Ph.D.; Deborah Bash, C.N.M.; Ruth Guyer, Ph.D ; Zoila Acevedo, R.N.. Ph.D.; Mary Anne Trause, Ph.D. Diane Reukauf, M.A. (Washington, D.C.: Acropolis Books Ltd., 1981.)

Growing Wisdom, Growing Wonder; Helping Your Child Learn From Birth Through Five Years, Gregg, Elizabeth. (New York: Macmillan Pub. Co., Inc., 1980.)

Choosing Toys For Children From Birth To Five, Kaban, Barbara. (New York: Schocken Books, Inc., 1979.)

Mother's Almanac, Kelly, Marguerite. (New York: Doubleday & Co., Inc., 1975.)

Total Baby Development, Koch, Jaroslav. (New York: Wyden Books, 1976.)

Growing Up With Your Children, Kohl, Herbert R. (Boston: Little Brown & Co., 1979.)

Your Baby & Child From Birth To Age Five, Leach, Penelope. (New York: Knopf, Alfred A., Inc., 1978.)

Guiding Your Child To A More Creative Life, Maynard, Fredelle Bruser. (New York: Doubleday & Co., Inc., 1973.)

Touching: The Human Significance Of The Skin, Montagu, Ashley. (New York: Harper & Row Pubs., Inc., 1978.)

The First Twelve Months of Life, Princeton Center for Infancy and Early Chiildhood. Parenting Advisor. (Princeton, N.J.: Grosset and Dunlap, 1971.)

The Second Twelve Months of Life, Princeton Center for Infancy and Early Childhood. Parenting Advisor. (Princeton, N.J.: Grosset and Dunlap, 1977.)

Baby & Child Care, Spock, Benjamin. (New York: Hawthorn Books, 1976.)

What Every Child Would Like His Parents To Know, Salk, Lee. (New York: Warner Paperback Library, 1974.)

Father's Almanac, Sullivan, S. Adams. (New York: Doubleday & Co., Inc., 1980.)

The World Of The Gifted Child, Vail, Priscilla. (New York: Walker & Co., 1979.)

Your Young Child And You, Weisberger, Eleanor. (New York: Dutton, E.P., 1979.)

About Children and Parents *(ages 5-10 yrs.)*

Your 5 Year Old; Your 6 Year Old, Ames, Louise. (New York: Delacorte Press, 1979.)

Teaching Your Child to Learn from Birth to School Age, Arnold, Arnold. (Englewood Cliffs, N.J.: Prentice-Hall, Inc., 1971.)

Whole Child, Whole Parent, Berends, Polly. (New York: Harper & Row Pubs., Inc., 1975.)

Your Child's Self-Esteem, the Key to His Life, Briggs, Dorothy. (New York: Doubleday & Co., Inc., 1970.)

Child's Body; A Parents' Manual, Diagram Group. (New York: Paddington Press, Ltd., 1977.)

Children the Challenge, Dreikurs, Rudolf. (New York: Hawthorn Books, 1964.)

How to Raise Independent and Professionally Successful Daughters, Dunn, Rita. (Englewood Clifs, N.J.: Prentice-Hall, Inc., 1977.)

Early Adolescents; Understanding and Nurturing Their Development, Cohen, M.D., ed. (Washington: Assoc. For Childhood Education, International, 1978.)

Child from Five to Ten Rev. Ed., Gessell, Arnold. (New York: Harper and Row Pub., Inc., 1977.)

P.E.T. Parent Effectiveness Training, the No-Lose Program for Raising Responsible Children, Gordon, Thomas. (New York: Wyden Books, 1970.)

Growing Up Free; Raising Your Child in the 80's, Pogrebin, Letty Cottin. (New York: McGraw-Hill Book Co., 1980.)

Help Me Learn. A Handbook for Teaching Children from Birth to Third Grade, Rice, Mary. (Englewood Cliffs, N.J.: Prentice-Hall, Inc., 1979.)

Children's Doctor, Smith, Lendon. (Englewood Cliffs, N.J.: Prentice-Hall, Inc., 1979.)

About Play and Learning *(to age 5)*

Playgroup Handbook, Broad, Laura P. and Nancy T. Butterworth. (New York: St. Martin's Press, Inc., 1974.)

Creative Movement for the Developing Child, Cherry, Clare. (Belmont, CA: Pitman Learning, Inc., 1971.)

I Saw A Purple Cow, Cole, Ann. (Boston: Little Brown & Co., 1972.)

Early To Learn, Crandall, Joy M. (New York: Dodd, Mead & Co., 1974.)

Child Learning Through Child Play, Gordon, Ira J. (New York: St. Martin's Press Inc., 1972.)

Games Babies Play, Hagstrom Julie and Joan Morrill. (Darby, N.H.: Addison-Wesley, 1979.)

Learning Through Play, Marzollo, Jean. (New York: Harper Row Pubs., Inc., 1974.)

Games for the Very Young, Matterson, Elizabeth. (New York: American Heritage, 1971.)

While You're At It; 200 Ways to Help Children Learn, Nassau Co., N.Y. (New York: Reston Pub. Co. 1976.)

Kids Are Natural Cooks, Parents Nursery School. (Boston: Houghton Mifflin, 1971.)

Whole Baby Catalog, Ross, Kathy Roberts. (New York: Sterling, 1977.)

Preparing Your Preschooler for Reading, Sparkman, Brandon and Jane Saul. (New York: Schocken Books, Inc., 1977.)

Resources, Learning Aids, and Sources for Activities

(ages 3-10 yrs.)

The Other Side of the Elephant—Theater Activities for Classroom Learning, Allen, June. (Buffalo: D.O.K. Publishers, 1977.)

Workjobs for Parents: Activity-centered Learning in the Home, Baratta-Lorton, Mary. (Darby, N.H.: Addison-Wesley, 1975.)

Bag of Tricks—Instructional Activities and Games, Blake, Janet. (Denver: Love Pub. Co., 1976.)

Great Perpetual Learning Machine; Being a Stupendous Collection of Ideas, Games, Experiments, Activities, and Recommendations for Further Exploration, Blake, Jim. (Boston: Little, Brown & Co., 1976.)

The Whole Kids Catalog, Cardozo, Peter. (New York: Bantam Books Inc., 1975.)

Scamper-Games for Imagination Development, Eberle, Robert. (Buffalo: D.O.K. Publishers, 1977.)

28 Ways to Help Your Child Be a Better Reader, Gambrell, Linda B. (Reading Education Inc., 1977.)

Learning for Little Kids. A Parents' Sourcebook for the Years 3 to 8, Jones, Sandy. (Boston: Houghton Mifflin Co., 1979.)

Making Things: The Handbook of Creative Discovery, Wiseman, Ann. (Boston: Little Brown & Co., 1973.)

Yellow Pages of Learning Resources, Wurman, Richard. (Boston: M.I.T., 1972.)

Have A Hint?

Do you have a hint that is *not* included in this book? Please send it along to the address below. We're interested in more parent tricks-of-the-trade.

Be sure to include the name(s) of your child-testers when you submit your hints. The date is important, too. If there are any duplicates, we will give credit to the parent and child whose idea we receive first.

Please send your child-tested solutions to:

Kathleen Touw
c/o Acropolis Books
2400 17th St., N.W.
Washington, D.C. 20009

Index

Suggested Reading
Available at bookstores everywhere

If unavailable through your bookseller, you may order directly from the publisher, Acropolis Books. Ltd.

Listening Games
92 Listening & Thinking Activities
by Margaret John Maxwell

Listening is one of the most vital of all learning skills, but most children never really learn how. And, when you consider that they spend 50 to 75% of their classroom time listening to what their teacher is teaching, it's obvious that **LISTENING GAMES** is a much-needed book.

Listening abilities are learned, and **LISTENING GAMES** provides parents and teachers with 92 fun games and activities they can play with children to teach them how. These games can be played at home, in the car, in the classroom. Little or no materials, besides this book, are needed. The games are geared to preschool through elementary school, for groups or individuals.

ISBN 87491-619-4/$9.95 quality paper
208 pages, 8-1/2 x 11, illustrated

Living And Learning With Children
301 Imaginative Games & Activities
for Young Children   by Paula Jorde

Here is a book full of imaginative activities you can play and do with your young children. Not only are they full-of-fun activities, but they will teach your three to six-year-old the beginnings of science, art, sensory awareness, music, math, reading and health.

From getting ready to read to what's cooking, all the materials for these activities are inexpensive and available at a local dime store, grocery store or right in the home.

Charmingly illustrated, with wholesome enticing recipes and a bibliography of "Helpful Books," this activity book will provide you and your children with hours of fun and learning.

ISBN 87491-289-X/$6.95 quality paper
96 pages, 8-1/2 x 11, fully illustrated

The Great Whale Book

by Dr. John E. Kelly
with Scott Mercer and Steve Wolf

Whales may be our closest marine relative, but modern whaling practices are threatening their very existence.

Now **THE GREAT WHALE BOOK** brings these warmblooded creatures out of the depths, describing their evolution, their physiology and behavior, and the history of our relationship with them.

Through delightful illustrations and photographs, history and zoology, learn how whales are persisting in the present battle between commercial whalers and those who want to protect the last of these beautiful creatures.

Published in cooperation with the Whale Protection Fund/Center for Environmental Education Inc., a portion of the royalties will go toward protecting the great whales and their marine habitat. Includes complete field guide to the whales of North America.

ISBN 87491-468-X/$7.95 quality paper
124 pages, 8 x 9, illustrations and photographs

The Way Of The Dolphin

by Dr. Michael Fox
illustrated by Betty J. Lewis

Now children can explore the world of one of the most intelligent creatures, the dolphin. They'll marvel at the dolphin's intricate way of communicating through a special "sonar" sense as they witness the birth of Nick-Nick and follow him through a series of both whimsical and perilous dolphin adventures. Whether fathoms below the sea, escaping from a school of killer whales, or cavorting on the foamy surface with a fisherman and his son — Nick-Nick, Teeka, Tiktik and their cousins are a continual source of wonder for children.

And Dr. Michael Fox, a well known proponent of animal rights and ethics, makes children aware of how mankind needlessly imperils his friend, the dolphin.

Dr. Michael W. Fox is Director of the Institute for the Study of Animal Problems, a division of the Humane Society of the United States. He is the author of numerous books, including *On the Fifth Day* (Acropolis, 1978), *Dr. Fox's Fables* (Acropolis, 1980), and *The Touchlings* (Acropolis 1981).

ISBN 87491-466-3/$7.95 hardcover
64 pages, 8 x 9, fully illustrated

Model of the United States Capitol

rendered by Robert Merritt

History comes alive when children put together this exact scaled replica of the U.S. Capitol — "the symbol of the power of the people," praised Nathaniel Hawthorne after a visit in 1862.

Now today's children can discover the fascinating history of this beautiful building, as they reconstruct its seven sections, the first begun in 1793, the last just completed in 1962.

Die-cut for easy assembly, this intriguing kit contains 1 in. to 32 ft. scaled parts for building a 24 in x 8-1/2 in. x 9 in. Capitol building. Complete with illustrated instructions and historical accounts, it makes an exciting educational activity for children 12 years and up (and that includes you!).

ISBN 87491-469-8/$11.95 per kit

Dr. Fox's Fables:
Lessons from Nature

by Dr. Michael Fox

Dr. Michael Fox, popular author and nationally-syndicated columnist of "Ask Your Vet," has put his vast knowledge of animal behavior and love of animals into this new children's book, *Dr. Fox's Fables: Lessons from Nature.*

In *Dr. Fox's Fables,* Dr. Fox lets his charmingly characterized animals teach children much about themselves and their environment, and how to protect and respect it. His animals are not "furry people," however, and are meant to teach children about the real world of nature. Thus, each fable adds to children's sense of wonder and kinship with animal life to give them a lifelong respect and reverence for all animals, including human beings.

ISBN 87491-291-1/$9.95 hardcover
ISBN 87491-516-3/$4.95 quality paper
124 pages, 8 x 9, illustrated, Grades 3-5

TOUCHLINGS, THE

The Adventures of the Fantasy Creatures that Live on Love, Sunshine and Giving. By Dr. Michael W. Fox. If you thought the Gnomes were loveable, wait until you meet the Touchlings! Children and adults will be inspired by this tender story. Includes full color Touchling poster. See page 19.
ISBN 87491-293-8/$7.95 hardcover

HOW TO HELP YOUR CHILD EAT RIGHT

By Antoinette Hatfield and Peggy Stanton. Tells every mother how to get her child off junk food and onto healthy, well-balanced diets. Nutrition information, menu plans, recipes, clues to entice your reticent eater and amusing and helpful anecdotes from other mothers.
ISBN 87491-253-9/$4.95 quality paper

FATHER BOOK, THE:

Pregnancy and Beyond. By members of the Alliance for Perinatal Research & Services Inc. The Father Book is a thorough, easy-to-read sympathetic guide for fathers to the biology, issues and joys of pregnancy, childbirth and fatherhood. See page 4.
ISBN 87491-618-6/$17.50 hardcover
ISBN 87491-422-1/$8.95 quality paper

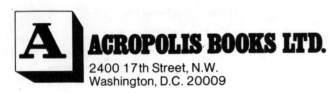